DON TROIANI'S CIVIL WAR
Militia & Volunteers

Art by Don Troiani
Text by Earl J. Coates, Michael J. McAfee, and Don Troiani

STACKPOLE
BOOKS

Copyright © 2002 by Stackpole Books, Images © 2002 by Don Troiani
Introduction © 2006 by Stackpole Books

Published in paperback in 2006 by
STACKPOLE BOOKS
5067 Ritter Road
Mechanicsburg, PA 17055
www.stackpolebooks.com

Printed in China

10 9 8 7 6 5 4 3 2 1

FIRST EDITION

For free information about the artwork and limited edition prints of Don Troiani, contact:

Historical Art Prints
P.O. Box 660
Southbury, CT 06488
203-262-6560
www.historicalartprints.com

For information on licensing images in this book, visit www.historicalimagebank.com

Library of Congress Cataloging-in-Publication Data

Troiani, Don.
    [Don Troiani's regiments and uniforms of the Civil War. Selections]
    Don Troiani's Civil War militia and volunteers / art by Don Troiani ; text by Earl J. Coates, Michael J. McAfee, and Don Troia.— 1st ed.
        p. cm.
    Reprints a section of the author's Don Troiani's regiments and uniforms of the Civil War. Mechanicsburg, PA : Stackpole Books, c2002.
      ISBN-13: 978-0-8117-3319-9
      ISBN-10: 0-8117-3319-X
      1. United States—Militia—History—Civil War, 1861–1865—Pictorial works. 2. United States—Militia—Uniforms—History—19th century—Pictorial works. 3. Confederate States of America. Army—Pictorial works. 4. Confederate States of America—Militia—Uniforms—Pictorial works. 5. Soldiers—United States—History—19th century—Pictorial works. 6. Soldiers—Confederate States of America—History—Pictorial works. 7. United States. Army—Uniforms—History—19th century—Pictorial works. 8. Confederate States of America. Army—Uniforms—Pictorial works. 9. United States—History—Civil War, 1861–1865—Regimental histories. 10. United States—History—Civil War, 1861–1865—Pictorial works. I. Title: Civil War militia and volunteers. II. Coates, Earl J. III. McAfee, Michael J. IV. Title.

E492.7.T76 2006
973.7'8—dc22
                                        2005027475

INTRODUCTION

THIS BOOK AND THE OTHERS IN THIS SERIES ARE taken from the larger volume *Don Troiani's Regiments and Uniforms of the Civil War* to provide a less expensive reference source for those interested in specific areas of Civil War uniforms. The subject of Civil War militia and volunteer uniforms could not be comprehensively covered in even twenty volumes like this one, but this publication will provide a good overview.

During the course of the war, more than a thousand regiments existed, comprising many more thousands of companies. Sometimes, different companies within the same regiment wore their own distinctive clothing. To confound things further, the uniform of a specific company might not have been the attire they actually wore into battle. Many were photographed in their finest outfits, but when duty called, they sensibly switched to simpler and more practical dress. At battles such as First Manassas, some regiments laid aside their showy uniforms and marched onto the field stripped down to their shirtsleeves. It was not until mid-1862 that uniformity of dress in both armies began to take shape.

My longtime friends, Earl J. Coates and Michael J. McAfee, represent the pinnacle of their fields in research, and working with them has always been an enjoyable and enriching experience. Contributing authors Tom Arliskis and David M. Sullivan, also leaders in their areas of study, presented fresh information and ideas. Working with primary source materials, period photography, and original artifacts gave us the opportunity to explore the dress of many units from a multidimensional perspective. Equally important was the wise counsel offered by some of the great Civil War collectors and students of material culture: James C. Frasca, John Henry Kurtz, Paul Loane, Dean Nelson, Michael O'Donnell, and John Ockerbloom, among many others. Their decades of practical hands-on experience provided knowledge that cannot be "book learned."

Posing fully dressed models for all the studies in the book also opened the vista of seeing what some of this stuff really looked like on the soldier. Reading about it is one thing; seeing it is quite another.

As the main topic is uniforms, we have not explored firearms or edged weapons as they are exhaustively covered by many other books. We have touched on accoutrements but not in anything approaching complete coverage, selecting mostly items that augmented illustrated uniforms.

In researching the figure studies, the authors consulted every available source. Despite our more than a hundred years of combined study, we recognize that there's a good chance that another interesting nugget of new or conflicting data, perhaps from an unpublished account or collection, could surface after this book's publication. But that is the way of historical research and, indeed, one of the facets that makes it both frustrating and fascinating. To those who are disappointed that a favorite regiment has been left out, please forgive me, I'll try to get to it in the future!

Don Troiani
Southbury, Connecticut

ACKNOWLEDGMENTS

I DEDICATE THIS BOOK TO MY FATHER, DOMINICK H. Troiani (1916–2005), 258th Field Artillery, HQ Company, 95th Infantry Division, who served his country in France and Germany in 1944–45. His war stories got me interested in all this as a child. I also dedicate it to all the gallant servicemen and women who continue to defend our country on a daily basis.

I owe a debt of gratitude to my distinguished friends Earl J. Coates and Michael J. McAfee, two of the greatest gurus on the subject of Civil War uniforms, who graciously tolerated all my ceaseless questions and, as always, shared the fruits of a lifetime research with me. They are genuinely "national treasures." Particular thanks to contributing authors Tom Arliskis, who provided important primary information on Western units, and David Sullivan renowned authority on Civil War marines.

Special credit to renowned Civil War author-photographer Michael O'Donnell for taking many of the fine color photos of artifacts for this book, and to Tracy Studios of Southbury, Connecticut.

The following individuals and institutions also contributed to the creation of this book: Gil Barrett, Bruce Bazelon, Carl Borick, Robert Braun, William Brayton, Major William Brown, William L. Brown III, Christopher Bryant, Rene Chartrand, Charles Childs, Dr. Michael Cunningham, Ray Darida, Dr. David Evans, William Erquitt, Robin Ferit, James C. Frasca, Joseph Fulginiti, Fred Gaede, Holly Hageman, Charles Harris, Randy Hackenburg, Gary Hendershott, Bruce Hermann, Steven Hill, Robert Hodge, Mark Jaeger, Les Jensen, James L. Kochan, Robert K. Krick, Michael Kramer, John Henry Kurtz, John P. Langellier, William Lazenby, Claude Levet, Paul C. Loane, Edward McGee, Bob McDonald, Steven McKinney, Howard M. Madaus, Michael P. Musick, Dean Nelson, Donna O'Brien, John Ockerbloom, Stephen Osmun, Col. J. Craig Nannos, Dean Nelson, Larry Page, Andrew Pells, Ron Palm, Nicholas Picerno, the late Brian Pohanka, Cricket Pohanka, Kenneth Powers, Shannon Pritchard, Pat Ricci, Steven Rogers, Nancy Dearing Rossbacher, A. H. Seibel Jr., Mark Sherman, Sam Small, Wes Small, James R. H. Spears, Steve Sylvia, Brendan Synonmon, William Synonmon, David Sullivan, Donald Tharpe, Mike Thorson, Warren Tice, Ken Turner, William A. Turner, Cole Unson, James Vance, Michael Vice, Gary Wilkensen, Don Williams, and Michael J. Winey.

The Booth Museum of Western Art, Cartersville, Georgia; Confederate Memorial Hall, New Orleans; Charleston Museum, Charleston, South Carolina; Connecticut Historical Society; Connecticut State Library; New York State Collection; Pamplin Historical Park and the National Museum of the Civil War Soldier; Middlesex County Historical Society; The Company of Military Historians; the Nelsonian Institute; *North South Trader* magazine; The Horse Soldier; The Union Drummer Boy; and the West Point Museum, United States Military Academy.

Militia and Early Volunteers

THE CONTRIBUTIONS OF THE AMERICAN MILITIA to the Civil War are largely unrecognized. The first troops to respond to the call for war, both North and South, came from the states' organized volunteer militias. Militia-trained officers and enlisted men moved to command positions in the newly recruited volunteer regiments because of their prior military training and social position in their communities as units were raised locally. Some militia regiments even served throughout the war with the volunteer armies. It was the American militia system that in many ways set the entire tone for the raising of the volunteer armies that ultimately fought the war.

In the chaos of the early days of the war, several units claimed "firsts." Clearly it was the militia of the South that first went to war. Militiamen throughout the South began seizing Federal arsenals and forts as their states declared they were seceding from the Union. In Charleston, South Carolina, the hotbed of secession, there was a well-organized volunteer militia, completely uniformed and equipped, its weapons largely drawn from the Federal government's support of the state militias. In fact, the cadets of the Citadel, one of the most celebrated military academies of the South, may actually be entitled to the claim of opening hostilities by firing upon a Union supply ship, the *Star of the West,* on January 9, 1861. South Carolina's militia had been called into service by Gov. Francis W. Pickens on December 17, 1860, and prompted the move of the Federal garrison from Fort Moultrie to the unfinished Fort Sumter. By January 1861, the South Carolina militia had been recruited to full strength and had effectively besieged the small garrison of Federal troops at Fort Sumter. The die was now cast, and the hand that cast it was that of a state militia force.

The American militia system originated in the "trained bands" of the colonial era. These groups had their origin in the English tradition that free men were entitled, as well as obligated, to participate in their own defense. Colonists armed and trained themselves for the common defense from Native Americans and foreign invaders. By 1860, the trained bands had become the states' volunteer militias. By law, all able-bodied white males of appropriate age had been required to be part of the enrolled or common militia. As threat of attack by Native Americans or foreign invasion faded, however, so did the impetus to actively participate in the militia system.

By the 1830s, the annual assemblage of the common militia had been reduced to the level of a holiday celebration. Lampooned in cartoons and folk art, the image of the militia muster in the early nineteenth century was that of a drunken frolic, with the militiamen armed with sticks and umbrellas. This is the image that still pervades the common conception of the American militia system. It overlooks, however, the parallel growth of the volunteer militia companies

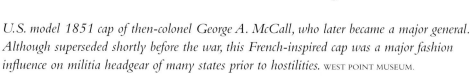

U.S. model 1851 cap of then-colonel George A. McCall, who later became a major general. Although superseded shortly before the war, this French-inspired cap was a major fashion influence on militia headgear of many states prior to hostilities. WEST POINT MUSEUM.

that began in the colonial era among a citizenry that was attracted to military life. The volunteer militia company was generally chartered by the state and composed of men who had volunteered to uniform and equip themselves at their own expense and submit to military discipline and drill to become a military organization. Every good-sized urban area had such companies. They were, to a large degree, social organizations, providing a sense of community and commitment, but some grew into respectable military units.

In the eighteenth and early nineteenth centuries, these volunteer companies were usually attached to the common militia paper regiments as "flank" or elite companies. Whereas the common militia officers were usually that in name only—the origin of the fabled "Kentucky colonel"—the officers of the volunteer companies frequently took their duties and obligations seriously, devoting time and often their own money to see that these military companies were properly trained and equipped. By the 1840s, the states were giving up on the common militia. The movement now known as Jacksonian democracy had advocated the abolition of the common militia as a social inequity, and Jacksonian politicians did nothing to encourage its invigoration or reform. Militia laws were ignored, and the common militia became virtually extinct. To fill the gap, the states rewrote their militia laws, replacing the common militia with the volunteer companies as the "active militia," while retaining on paper the manpower count of their citizenry as a potential militia body.

The volunteer militias, once completely drawn under state authority, often continued to demonstrate the individuality with which they had been conceived. They continued to wear their distinctive uniforms of their own design. These often reflected the origins of the company and ranged from the national blue of the American Guard of the 71st New York State Militia to the Irish green coatees of the Montgomery Guards of Charleston, South Carolina. The traditionalists, such as the 7th Regiment of New York City, often continued to wear gray. By the 1850s, however, as New York and other states tried to impose regimentalization upon what had previously been independent companies, uniforms became more standardized. In the North, dark blue frock coats and uniform caps of the Federal 1851 pattern were common. In the South, as in Virginia, gray frock coats and coatees were common, but as company, rather than regimental, uniforms. As late as the mid-1850s, the uniform in Georgia was half seriously said to be "a Shirt-collar and a pair of Spurs."[1] Yet the reformers had their way, and before the war began, much of the militia had been revitalized.

No state better typified the results of this reorganization than the state of New York. On the eve of the Civil War, New York's military force comprised some 19,000 rank and file, with a staff of 532 officers. These men were organized into a force of 62 active regiments. These ranged in size from smaller, rural regiments of 400 men to the elite 7th Regiment of New York City, with over 1,000 soldiers. Some were still armed with inadequate or antiquated weaponry, such as altered flintlocks, but efforts had been made to acquire better weapons, such as the M1855 rifle muskets and rifles of the 7th Regiment. When war began in 1861, New York had a militia force that could immediately be placed at Federal call.[2] In December 1860, the editor of the *Military Gazette*

Coat worn by Col. Elmer Ellsworth of the 11th New York Volunteers when killed on May 24, 1861, in Alexandria, Virginia. After receiving his uniform from the tailor, Ellsworth stated prophetically, "It is in this suit I shall die." The coat bears the damage of the shotgun blast in the chest, although the bloodstains were washed out many years ago. COLLECTION OF NEW YORK STATE DIVISION OF MILITARY AND NAVAL AFFAIRS.

Trousers with red-edged gold stripe worn by Col. Elmer Ellsworth at the time of his death. COLLECTION OF NEW YORK STATE DIVISION OF MILITARY AND NAVAL AFFAIRS.

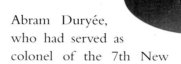

Forage cap patterned on the U.S. model 1839 worn by Capt. H. M. Nelson of Virginia's Clark Cavalry before the war and possibly as a captain of the 1st Virginia Cavalry at Manassas in 1861. There appears to have been a six-pointed star (now missing) on the front.
TROIANI COLLECTION.

wrote, "Every day brings news of Military preparations at the South, and we sincerely hope that it will only do for the Southern Militia what the Anti-Rent War preparations did for this State—enlist their best men, and raise a fine force, ready for use against a foreign foe, or preserve internal tranquility, but never against their brethren of other States, or against the Union!"[3]

Thus when the war began, the militias of both North and South provided the first men in service. Whether the 7th of New York, "the regiment that saved the capitol," or the Charleston Zouave Cadets at Fort Sumter, militiamen usually began the great American conflict dressed in their militia uniforms. The first Massachusetts troops to leave the state wore their individual company uniforms, with only gray overcoats procured by the state's governor John Andrews for uniformity. The men of the 7th New York went to Washington in natty gray fatigue uniforms of jackets and chasseur caps. The first Rhode Island troops wore loose blue flannel smocks with gray trousers in place of their militia uniforms. The South Carolina forces at Charleston ranged from the gray and red of the Charleston Zouave Cadets to the green smocks of riflemen. Together they presented a veritable military kaleidoscope of uniforms.

Whereas the militias could provide the first troops for what was to become a long and protracted struggle, the militia force itself was incapable of sustaining the war effort. On May 3, 1861, Pres. Abraham Lincoln called for 42,000 three-year volunteers and 22,000 more men for the Regular service. With the defeat at Bull Run, he called for an additional 500,000 volunteers. Confederate president Jefferson Davis began accepting volunteers as early as February 1861, and after a series of calls for volunteers, the South began conscription in April 1862. North and South alike, these volunteers represented a new breed of soldiers.

Because the central governments in 1861 lacked the structure and resources to form these volunteers into viable military units, that task was left to the individual states. Each state had an allotted number of regiments to provide, even though in the first days there were generally more volunteers than required. Following the militia tradition, regiments were generally recruited by a central prospective unit commander. Especially in the first days, these men were frequently from the militia system. One of the war's premier regiments, the 5th New York, Duryée's Zouaves, was the creation of Col.

Abram Duryée, who had served as colonel of the 7th New York State Militia Regiment from 1849 to 1859. Robert G. Shaw, colonel of the 54th Massachusetts Volunteer Infantry, the famed African-American regiment, had first gone to war as a private in the same regiment when the 7th marched to "save" Washington in April 1861.

In a few cases, whole militia regiments volunteered for war service. The 2nd, 9th, 14th, 20th, and 79th Regiments of New York State Militia became, respectively, the 82nd, 83rd, 84th, 80th, and 79th Volunteer Regiments during the war. More frequently, a militia regiment became the recruiting core for volunteers. The 6th New York brought forth the 66th New York, which had as its lieutenant colonel Samuel Zook of the old 6th Regiment. Zook later became colonel of the 57th New York and died at Gettysburg as a brigadier general. After the 69th New York Militia Regiment served at First Bull Run, it returned to New York City, where it raised a volunteer 69th Regiment, the core of the famed Irish Brigade, and later the 182nd New York of the Corcoran Brigade. The link between the militia and volunteer regiments in the early days of the war was especially strong.

Although militia troops could go to war in their own privately purchased uniforms, providing uniforms for the influx of civilian volunteers completely strained the resources of even the prosperous and industrial North. Jackets were manufactured in stopgap fashion throughout the North. In New York, they were to have eight-button fronts and be of blue cloth, but immediately jackets of shoddy gray were accepted to meet the demands of uniforming the new recruits. In Pennsylvania, jackets with nine-button fronts made of cloth of varying shades of gray and light blue were issued to the first volunteers.[4] Jackets of blue and gray were common issue throughout Ohio, Indiana, and Illinois as well.

In the South, the first regiments of new volunteers wore locally manufactured uniforms often based upon those of the militia. The Virginia militia companies in their distinctive uniforms were joined into regiments lacking in uniformity. In Louisiana, with the urbane center of New Orleans, there were uniformed Zouaves and chasseurs in tribute to the Creole heritage of the city. The blue-coated Washington Artillery of that same city, as trim and proper as any Northern militia unit, went to war in gray jackets in the East, while its Western companies served in blue denim jackets and trousers. Southern volunteers went to war in blue as well as gray, just as in the North. Some states devised distinctive uniforms. In North Carolina, the regulation uniform for state troops was a six-button sack coat of gray with black stripes on the shoulder for infantry, red for artillery, and yellow for cavalry. In 1861, Mississippi troops were to wear shirts of distinctive colors—red for infantry, gray for artillery, and blue for cavalry. Their hats were to be black felt, looped up on three sides. With each state, and often each locality, providing its own clothing at the war's start, the diversity was unending. Only later would some uniformity be established with the issue of uniforms produced in regional clothing depots.

This mixture of blues and grays within both the Union and Confederate forces, along with the colorful Zouave and other distinctive uniforms common to both sides, inevitably led to confusion on the battlefront. At Big Bethel in June 1861, the gray uniforms of the 3rd New York caused other Union soldiers to fire upon them.

The problem had been foreseen, and attempts for easy identification were attempted without great success. As early as May 1861, several Southerners had suggested badges for identification. From New Orleans, a "C. Schumacker" offered distinctive arm badges. A lady, F. B. Johnston of Salem, Virginia, offered to make "a rosette of red and blue ribbon" for the same purpose. In August 1861, Stonewall Jackson's men adopted their own device—"a Sherr [sheer?] strip of white cotton cloth about an inch wide and six long attached to the top of the cap"—as a means of distinction.[5] In the North, the gray-clad 47th New York was ordered to wear "a broad stripe of red, white and blue" on the left sleeve to distinguish "Union troops when on the field of battle." None of these devices was ever truly successful, but in the end, the economy of mass production solved these problems as the blue and the gray sorted themselves out.

Neither professional soldiers nor citizen soldiers, the volunteers of 1861 personified the American nation. They were a cross section of a boisterous and rambunctious populace about to be forged into a new nation in the crucible of war.

Prewar Connecticut militia shako of an unidentified unit, bearing the state seal and infantry hunting horn device. This item was made by John A. Baker of New York City, who supplied headgear to state militias across the country in the prewar years. MIDDLESEX COUNTY HISTORICAL SOCIETY.

Emblazoned in gold embroidery on a blue velvet band on this forage cap, the legend "Scott Life Guard" proclaimed to all the title of the 4th New York Volunteers. It was worn by Capt. William B. Parisen, who served with the unit from April 1861 until its muster out in August 1863. TROIANI COLLECTION.

6TH REGIMENT, MASSACHUSETTS VOLUNTEER MILITIA, 1861

On the anniversary of the battles of Lexington and Concord, April 19, 1861, Massachusetts "minutemen" were again under fire. These militiamen had mustered on April 17, 1861, from their widely scattered homes in Middlesex and Essex Counties for the defense of the nation's capital. Their journey south had taken them through New York and New Jersey to Philadelphia. The 6th Massachusetts left that city for Washington at 1 A.M. on the nineteenth, but its route was through Baltimore, and that city was in turmoil, with secessionists vowing to stop the passage of reinforcements to the Capitol.

Col. Edward F. Jones of the 6th simply stated, "My orders are to reach Washington at the earliest possible moment, and I shall go on." Eventually six of the regiment's companies had safely traversed Baltimore, but the last four—C, I, D, and L—were trapped by a murderous mob. Brickbats and bullets flew at these unfortunate soldiers, who fought back, firing at rioters who were foolhardy enough to openly attack. Even Baltimore's mayor, marching with the column, joined in, taking an M1855 rifle musket from a fallen soldier to shoot his attacker.

When the regiment reunited, four men had been killed and thirty-six officers and men wounded. The march through Baltimore was not a battle, but the blood had been drawn. Their arrival in Washington was described by the *Washington Evening Star:* "The Massachusetts volunteers are provided with the dark-gray overcoat, water-proof knapsacks and haversacks, regulation caps and new rifle muskets. Each man is provided with two flannel shirts and two pairs of drawers and stockings. Many of them being hastily recruited, were not fully uniformed. The uniformed companies have black pants, with red and orange stripes down the sides, and dark blue infantry coats." Clad in state-purchased overcoats and militia shakos, the 6th Massachusetts had gone to war as citizen soldiers. They were true descendants of their Revolutionary ancestors.

Private, Maryland Guard, 1861

The Maryland Guard was organized and raised in Baltimore in late 1859. The guard was formed as a battalion of four companies and became part of the 53rd Regiment of the Maryland Militia. Over the next months, two more companies were added. As with many of the finely dressed militia companies in the large cities of the eastern United States, the Maryland Guard was composed of young men of the best class. An advertisement that appeared in the local newspapers, such as the *Baltimore American and Commercial Advertiser,* touted the fact that the uniform each member was required to buy was "simple and cheap," costing $42.68. Recruits were given three months to fully outfit themselves. The ad described the uniform as consisting of an overcoat; full chassseur uniform, which included a light blue flannel shirt with ornamental brass buttons, jacket and pantaloons trimmed with yellow, red cummerbund, and gaiters; cap; knapsack; blanket; body belt; and undress jacket. Both the full dress and undress uniforms were predominantly blue, except for the undress pantaloons, which were black. The belts were changed from white to black for parade and fatigue.

The color of the uniform doomed it to a short history. Secessionist sentiment ran high in Baltimore, and most of the Maryland Guard immediately cast their lot with the South when war came. Although the uniform of the Maryland Guard was short-lived, its style represents well the feeling and spirit during the months leading up to the war.

DAVID RANKIN, JR.

Many members of the battalion made their way to Richmond. Once there, they were outfitted by the state of Virginia. The uniform they received was described by one guardsman, James McHenry Howard, as "coarse gray, but very durable." The Maryland men were not destined to serve as a unit, however. Two companies were sent from Richmond to Winchester, Virginia, to form the nucleus of the Confederate 1st Maryland Regiment. Left behind was one company under Capt. J. Lyle Clarke, which became Company B, 21st Virginia Infantry, and served as such for the duration of the war. Both regiments saw extensive action with the Army of Northern Virginia.

7TH REGIMENT, NEW YORK STATE MILITIA, 8TH COMPANY, 1861

Few militia units have ever gained the fame of New York's 7th Regiment. In 1861, the 7th was considered the epitome of a militia unit. Whereas most state militias consisted of underorganized companies, each with distinctive uniforms, loosely coalesced into paper regiments, the 7th numbered a full 1,000 men with a regimental staff, even a surgeon and a chaplain. Before the war, in common with other New York militias, there was a company of cavalry and a mountain howitzer battery in the regiment as well.

Although called a "silk-stocking" regiment, it drew largely from New York City's burgeoning middle class, with young clerks, salesmen, and junior professionals filling its ranks as enlisted men. Its officers were mainly successful businessmen, with a dedication to the regiment that surpassed a hobby. Thus when President Lincoln called for volunteers in 1861, he expected the nation's militias to respond, and the 7th was the first to leave New York City. Gen. Winfield Scott felt that the 7th's national reputation made it ideal for the defense of the nation's capital, and it has been called the regiment that "saved the Capitol" because of its dramatic appearance on the streets of Washington, D.C., just as Lincoln despaired of troops. It was described as it marched in Washington: "The infantry is armed with improved regulation muskets [M1855 rifle muskets] and bayonets, the troop of horse with pistols and heavy swords,

Worsted epaulets for dress coatee worn by Lewis C. Parmelee of the 7th New York State Militia. TROIANI COLLECTION.

and the engineers with rifles [M1855] and sabre bayonets. Almost every man is armed with a pistol, including musicians and servants, and some have heavy dirks and knives."

Its gray fatigue uniforms were trimmed with black, a color combination chosen in the 1820s and retained by the regiment through the twentieth century. The white-buff belts supported the accoutrements of the men, which were supplemented with personal, nonissue blankets of various colors and designs. Gray knit sack coats, nicknamed "Aspinwalls" after

their donor, were also worn in Washington. Their uniforms were never stained with the soil of combat, for the 7th did not go to Bull Run, returning to New York City and mustering out early in June 1861. That does not mean that these men saw no combat, however, for by war's end, 606 of these enlisted men and officers accepted commissions in various other organizations of the Regular army and volunteer forces. One of them was Pvt. Robert Gould Shaw, who later served as colonel of the 54th Massachusetts Volunteer Infantry.

Dress shako worn by Lewis C. Parmelee as a member of the 7th New York State Militia from 1859 until 1861. As an officer in the 2nd U.S. Sharpshooters, Parmalee was killed at Antietam while capturing a Confederate flag, an act for which he was awarded the Medal of Honor. TROIANI COLLECTION.

A .69-caliber cartridge box made by L. S. Baker and used by Parmelee in the 7th New York State Militia before the war. The heavily varnished flap bears the gilt brass device "NG," for National Guard. TROIANI COLLECTION.

1ST REGIMENT SOUTH CAROLINA RIFLES, 1861

The 1st Regiment South Carolina Rifles was raised in the extreme western part of the state and was the first South Carolina regiment mustered into Confederate service. As with many early Confederate regiments, its first uniform was dark blue trimmed in green, the traditional color for a rifle regiment, although the arms supplied it by the state were old smoothbore muskets. In June 1861, the Confederate government published regulations requiring its troops to be uniformed in gray. Following this, dress of the 1st Rifles was changed to conform. The green trim was retained, as were the hats with rifle insignia. The arms were upgraded, but only to the more modern M1842 musket. The regiment did not obtain rifled arms until well after it had joined the Army of Northern Virginia.

The 1st Rifles was the first South Carolina regiment to change its original enlistment from one year to the open-ended "for the war" required by the Confederate government. This decision ordained that the men of the 1st Rifles would see action in all the major engagements of the famed army in which they served. By the fall of 1862, the original uniforms of many of the enlisted men had begun to wear out, and regimental records show a rapid replacement by uniforms with jackets rather than coats. At the battle of Fredericksburg, December 13, 1862, the 1st Rifles sustained heavy casualties. Among the mortally wounded was Ordnance Sgt. H. Berry Arnold, who had been first sergeant of Company L. Sergeant Arnold

PRIVATE COLLECTION

died at Chimborazo Hospital in Richmond, leaving behind clothing and items that most certainly reflect what he brought with him from home, including all or part of his original uniform, as recorded in the Compiled Service Records:

1 - coat	2 - pair socks
1 - vest	1 - pair boots
1 - pair pants	1 - knapsack
2 - pair drawers	1 - pocket book
3 - shirts	1 - silver pencil and gold pen
1 - hat	$102.40

The 1st South Carolina Rifles served the Confederacy until the end of the war, seeing action in nearly every important battle fought by the Army of Northern Virginia. At Appomattox, only a surviving 157 officers and men were present. They could return knowing that no Confederate regiment could boast a more gallant record of service.

DRIVE THEM TO WASHINGTON

The battle of First Manassas on July 21, 1861, made it painfully evident that the war, which had initially been expected to be a short one, was likely to extend at least into the following year. Also evident was the fact that unless some effort was made to dress both armies in distinctive uniforms, there would be continued instances of soldiers from the same command firing on friendly forces. It was during this battle that Thomas J. Jackson received his famed nickname of "Stonewall," at the head of the brigade that would share that name. No clearer picture of the lack of uniformity exists than that of Jackson at the head of the 4th and 27th Virginia Regiments, but dressed in the uniform of a colonel of the Federal army. Arrayed behind him, ready to drive the Yankees from the field, his Virginians were virtually indistinguishable from many on the opposite side of the battlefield. Most had received locally made uniforms, many wearing battle shirts that were not uniform even within the same regiment. To add to the problem, inspection reports from the end of June showed that during the short time since leaving home, the soldiers' clothing had become worn, further blurring distinction between Northern and Southern troops.

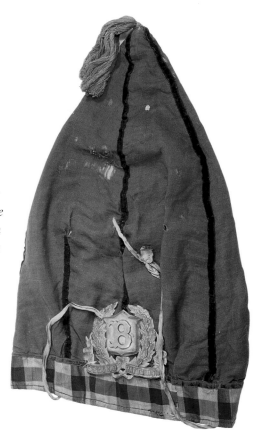

Influenced by the dress in Garibaldi's campaigns of liberation, this distinctive Sicilian style headgear was popular in the South during the opening months of the war. It was often worn in company with a hat or kepi. This rare specimen bears a brass badge marked "8th Regt, 2nd Batt."

COLLECTION OF NEW YORK STATE DIVISION OF MILITARY AND NAVAL AFFAIRS.

PRIVATE, COMPANY I, 4TH VIRGINIA INFANTRY C.S.A., THE LIBERTY HALL VOLUNTEERS

Civil War regiments, and the various companies they comprised, tended to be made up of men from the same general geographic area or who shared a common heritage. Company I of the 4th Virginia Infantry was composed primarily of students from Virginia's Washington College, which from 1776 to 1798 was known as Liberty Hall Academy. With obvious pride in their school, the young men who volunteered for the great adventure did so as the Liberty Hall Volunteers. Before the end of the academic year, the company they formed had been receiving military training from cadets of neighboring Virginia Military Institute. By the time they were mustered into Confederate service on June 2, 1861, to serve for a period of one year, the men of Washington College were considered a well-drilled command, at least by 1861 standards. But the young men learned quickly that cannonballs and bullets had no respect for academic achievement. At the battle of First Manassas, the men from Liberty Hall saw six of their number killed and several wounded.

The Liberty Hall Volunteer shown here is dressed as men of his company appeared on the field at Manassas in July 1861. His uniform consists of a battle shirt instead of a jacket, accoutrements described in the service records as "old and indifferent," and a .69-caliber smoothbore musket altered from flintlock to percussion. When originally outfitted, the company had no bayonet scabbards and no cap boxes, both of which were privately obtained and paid for by the company commander, Capt. James J. White.

DAVID RANKIN, JR.

Regimental returns of the 4th Virginia for the first three months of the war show that Company I was typical. The service records list six companies of the regiment as armed with the altered muskets, one with the cadet musket, and two with Harpers Ferry rifles, better known as Mississippi rifles. In every company, the uniforms were reported as "much worn and in bad condition."

On April 14, 1862, Company I was reorganized for the duration of the war, with the addition of forty-nine men from the militia and eleven transfers from other units, and it lost much of its academic flavor. The 4th Virginia served with the Army of Northern Virginia until the end of the war. It was organized along with the 2nd, 5th, 27th, and 33rd Virginia Regiments to make up the famous Stonewall Brigade, a fact that, as veterans, the men who had left school to fight for the Confederacy as members of the Liberty Hall Volunteers most certainly boasted of in years to come.

FLAT RIVER GUARD, COMPANY B, 6TH NORTH CAROLINA STATE TROOPS INFANTRY

With "military fever" running high in April 1861, the young men of Orange County, North Carolina, flocked to the colors in numbers sufficient to quickly raise two companies of infantry. One of these companies, the Flat River Guard, numbered fifty enlisted men under the command of Capt. Robert F. Webb. Through the efforts of the ladies of the county, the company was uniformed and prepared for war. Because North Carolina was a major textile manufacturing state, it is likely that the cloth for these uniforms was of local manufacture of what was termed "North Carolina gray cassimere," according to Frederick P. Todd in *American Military Equipage, 1851–1872.* The hat worn by the guards was likely issued by the state. It is similar to the U.S. regulation hat but bears the early-style hunting horn insignia, as well as the letters FRG.

In May, Captain Webb was ordered by the adjutant general of North Carolina to move his company to Raleigh. It was here that the guards were mustered as Company B, 6th North Carolina Infantry, commanded by Col. Charles Fisher, who, according to Richard W. Iobst in *The Bloody Sixth,* had determined to raise a regiment of "smiths, carpenters, masons, and engineers." Colonel Fisher had been a member of the North Carolina Senate and president of the North Carolina Railroad and was obviously a man of wealth. He supplied the regiment with knapsacks, bayonet scabbards, and canteens and was likely responsible for unique belt plate that was manufactured for, and proudly worn by, the men of his command.

The 6th Regiment was immediately sent to Virginia and assigned to the brigade commanded by Brig. Gen. Bernard E. Bee. It received its baptism of fire on the field of Manassas. The regiment charged Ricketts's and Griffin's Federal batteries and sustained heavy losses, not only from the batteries and their infantry support, but also from Confederate troops in their rear who fired into them. Among those killed was Colonel Fisher.

DAVID RANKIN, JR.

Clinch Rifles, Georgia Militia, April 1861

The Clinch Rifles were formed in Augusta, Georgia, in 1852. Named in honor of a hero of the War of 1812, Gen. Duncan Clinch, the company was typical of the numerous elite militia organizations that could be found in the large cities of the United States in the decade prior to the Civil War. These companies were often composed of the best and the brightest young men of the urban areas, most of whom had sufficient financial backing to outfit themselves in the height of military fashion.

Membership in the Clinch Rifles was both an honor and a privilege that was not granted lightly. A young man aspiring to membership would be voted on and was expected to pay dues, outfit himself in the company's uniform, and attend regular meetings. The purchase of one uniform was usually not enough, as style changes would dictate that those wishing to remain must be ready to conform to the decision of the majority. The meticulously kept minutes of the meetings of the Clinch Rifles show that on May 30, 1859, a resolution was adopted to "change the uniform by making the coat a frock coat." This was followed just over a year later in July 1860 by a decision to discuss a design for a new uniform. These uniforms would be tailor-made in Augusta. For those wishing to belong, peer pressure certainly was alive and well.

In keeping with the European tradition of green for riflemen, and adding an elegant gold braid trim, the Clinch Rifles' uniform made it a distinctive and easily recognized company. The new uniform was based in style, if not in color, on the latest issue of the Regular army. The French-style forage cap had been adopted by the Regulars in 1858 for fatigue purposes. The frock coat for full dress had replaced a similar, less practical pattern the same year. Whereas the Regulars would not wear the two items together, the decision to do so by the Clinch Rifles made for a smart and practical uniform by the standards of 1860.

Unlike many units raised in 1861 that bore the title of Rifles, the men of the Clinch Rifles were armed as a true rifle company, carrying the 1841 Mississippi rifle modified to use the deadly looking saber bayonet. These rifles had been issued by the state of Georgia, which had received them from the Federal government, which, under a law dating from 1808, had issued the various states arms for their militias. The belt, the U.S. rifle belt model of 1855 with an attached frog to hold the scabbard for the saber bayonet, also stood out as

unique to a rifle company. The cartridge box for the Mississippi rifle had no provision for a shoulder belt and was worn on the right side of the waist belt. Although the saber bayonet had the appearance of a formidable arm, it was not well liked by the men who used it. One primary reason was the fact that it made the arm difficult to load quickly when it was in place on the rifle. Another negative factor was the weight of the weapon, which, when added to the weight of a full cartridge box, added to the soldier's already significant burden.

Silver and star crescent badge belonging to Pvt. J. Macready of
Company A, 7th Louisiana, who enlisted at New Orleans
on April 22, 1861. WILLIAM ERQUITT COLLECTION.

ANDREW B. BOOTH, *RECORDS OF LOUISIANA SOLDIERS AND COMMANDS*
(SPARTANBURG, S.C.: REPRINT PUBLISHERS, 1984), 832.

Gray cloth-covered Virginia militia shako made by Wm. B. Richards of
Alexandria, Virginia, bearing a brass state seal. This pattern was used by
the Old Dominion Rifles, which became Company H of the 17th Virginia Infantry.
The January 31 and March 23, 1861, Alexandria Gazette described the manufacturer's
business: "Mr. Richards enjoys peculiar facilities for getting up military apparel and
has during the past winter completely uniformed several companies of our section of the
state and several from a distance." ANDREW PELLS COLLECTION.

A prewar South
Carolina die-stamped belt plate of a style in wide use
before and during the early part of the war by troops of
that state. The plate bears the state seal originally
designed in 1776, with the device of a palmetto tree,
hearkening back to the defense of Charleston Harbor
in 1776 when the palmetto trees at Fort Moultrie
absorbed the fire from British cannonballs.

WEST POINT MUSEUM.

Prewar coatee worn by Capt. Hugh Mortimer Nelson of
the Clark Cavalry of Virginia. In 1861, this unit formed
a company of the famed 1st Virginia Cavalry, commanded
by J. E. B. Stuart. TROIANI COLLECTION.

THE FIRST BATTLE FLAGS

As the summer of 1861 passed, it was evident that the war that had begun in April was not going to be over in the few months many had originally believed. Also evident was the fact that Confederate regiments needed a distinctive flag to be carried into battle—a flag that would be easily recognized at a distance on a smoke-shrouded field by friend and foe alike. The confusion and tragic instances of troops killed by friendly fire in some of the first battles had resulted in part from the wide variety of uniforms being worn and in part because the flags being carried could easily be mistaken for that of the enemy. By late fall, the problem of uniforms was on its way to being rectified, as the Richmond Clothing Depot and other facilities were now beginning to produce a uniform that, if not standard in the strictest sense, was at least distinct from that worn by the Union army. At the same time, there emerged a proud new banner that would eventually become one of the most enduring symbols of the Southern Confederacy. In November 1861, near Centreville, Virginia, the first issue of the new battle flag was made.

The officers receiving the flags included men whose names were already becoming household words in the Confederacy: Joseph E. Johnston, James Longstreet, Gustavus Smith, and Earl Van Dorn. The uniforms worn by these men reflected a mixture of Federal and Confederate regulations, with a generous dose of personal taste. According to Lt. Colin Selph, an officer on General Johnston's staff who was assigned the duty of obtaining the silk for these flags, they varied in color from light pink to red due to the unavailability of scarlet silk. Because of a scarcity of silk in the South, subsequent issues of the battle flag were made of scarlet bunting, which bore the strain of use in the field much better. It was not, after all, the type of material, but the cause the flags represented that made those who followed them into battle willing to sacrifice all in their defense.

Stiffened officer's kepi with gray satinette cloth covering and gold tape trimming. The design appears to have been based loosely on what was in fashion in Europe at the time. This cap belonged to Lt. William R. Macbeth of Company B, 16th Louisiana Battalion (Confederate Guards Response Battalion), who was killed on April 6, 1862. CONFEDERATE MEMORIAL HALL, CLAUDE LEVET PHOTOGRAPH.

3RD ALABAMA INFANTRY, COMPANY A, MOBILE CADETS, 1861

For the young men of the Mobile Cadets, the heady excitement of the first months of 1861 must then have seemed like a dream come true. Here at last was the opportunity to make the fantasies of military glory a reality. The company had been formed in 1845, and then as now contained some of the finest youth from the wealthiest families of Mobile, Alabama. Since the early days, the cadets, while excelling at military drill and target practice, had been little more than a social club. Now, with the Federal evacuation of Fort Sumter, the possibility of war seemed very real. So real, in fact, that the captain of the cadets was waiting in the telegraph office following the news of the evacuation when the call for volunteers was received. A return message was immediately sent to the Alabama governor offering the services of the Mobile Cadets to the Confederacy. Within days, the cadets moved to Montgomery, where they were designated

Frock coats were more prevalent in the Confederacy during the early part of the war, until economical considerations dictated a shift to jacket manufacture. This early specimen is believed to have been worn by a soldier in the 5th Louisiana Regiment. TROIANI COLLECTION.

Knit woolen smoking cap, or tam-o'-shanter, worn by Pvt. Edward N. Whittier of the 1st Rhode Island Detached Militia. Informal caps of all sorts were favored by troops during quiet moments in camp. TROIANI COLLECTION.

Company A, 3rd Regiment Alabama Infantry. The 3rd was the first Alabama command to leave the state for Virginia, where on May 4, 1861, at Lynchburg, they were mustered into Confederate service.

The early uniform of the Mobile Cadets had been patterned after the undress uniform of the U. S. Military Academy at West Point. Between the time the company was mustered into actual service and its movement to the seat of war, it had received more suitable attire consisting of cadet gray jackets with matching trousers and forage caps all trimmed in black. Probably while at Lynchburg, the cadets

received M1841 Mississippi rifles with saber bayonets, which were shipped to that point from Alabama's Mount Vernon Arsenal. From Lynchburg, the 3rd Alabama was ordered to Norfolk, Virginia, where it remained until the city was evacuated on May 5, 1862. The Mobile Cadets found the action they had looked for in the Seven Days' battles before Richmond. At Seven Pines and Malvern Hill, the 3rd Alabama lost a total of 367 men killed and wounded. At Malvern Hill, the dead of the 3rd Alabama included two Mobile Cadets, both killed bearing the regimental colors.

1st Rhode Island Detached Militia, 1861

Of all the volunteers and militiamen who gathered in Washington, D.C., in early 1861, few were so distinctly dressed as the Rhode Island troops of Col. Ambrose Burnside. Recruited from several militia companies and battalions, the 1st Rhode Island Detached Militia wore a simple blue overshirt or smock, gray trousers, and black-brimmed hats or blue chasseur caps. Often their caps sported the white linen covers called havelocks after the English general who sported

Wool flannel shirt blouse worn by Pvt. Edward N. Whittier of the 1st Rhode Island Detached Militia at the battle of Bull Run in 1861. Manufactured by the firm of Macullar, Williams, and Parker, they were merely shirts worn outside the trousers and adorned with small brass flower buttons. A company of carabineers armed with Burnside carbines wore rifle insignia on the sleeves. TROIANI COLLECTION.

ALAN H. ARCHAMBAULT, "THE FIRST REGIMENT RHODE ISLAND DETACHED MILITIA, 1861," *MILITARY HISTORIAN AND COLLECTOR* 53, NO. 3 (FALL 2001): 105–6.

Kepi worn by Pvt. Edward N. Whittier of the 1st Rhode Island Detached Militia at First Manassas. Originally dark blue, it has faded to a brownish hue because of the noncolorfast logwood dyes used by contractors. The color breakdown could occur rapidly, as attested to by one Union soldier who was quoted in the November 23, 1861, Boston Evening Journal *shortly after leaving home as saying that "the rusty gray pants and blue caps turned to reddish brown and are not particularly becoming."* TROIANI COLLECTION.

such devices in India. It was a simple and practical uniform shared with Rhode Island's other infantry regiment, the 2nd.

These militiamen marched to First Bull Run with Burnside, who was now a brigade commander. The line companies were armed with M1855 rifle muskets, but a special carbineer company formed for skirmishing was issued breech-loading carbines of Burnside's own design. It needed these arms, as it was thrust into the fighting early on, spearheading the assault on Matthew's Hill. Despite their valiant performance, by the end of the day's battle, the stalwart Rhode Islanders joined in the general withdrawal and eventual rout of the amateur Federal army.

11TH VIRGINIA INFANTRY, COMPANY E, THE LYNCHBURG RIFLES, JULY 1861

The use of battle shirts in place of jackets or coats was a common practice in many Confederate regiments in the early days of the war. These shirts could be produced with comparative ease by local tailors or ladies' sewing circles and presented the proud volunteers with a distinctive garb they could wear to meet the Yankees. Had the war lasted only the few weeks or months as predicted by many, this may have been the only uniform many Southern boys would have worn. However, fate and the Federal army determined otherwise, and these distinct and often colorful garments soon disappeared. By the end of the summer of 1861, the image of the ragged Confederate was a reality. Uniforms made of cloth that would hold up well in civilian use started before long to disintegrate under the harsh reality of military service. These were soon replaced by uniforms made in Confederate government facilities from Richmond to Houston, Texas.

Company E, 11th Virginia Infantry, the Lynchburg Rifles, contained many faculty members and students from Lynchburg College. The company was commanded by Capt. James E. Blankenship, who had been a professor of mathematics and a member of the school's military department. Captain Blankenship was certainly qualified by education to command, as he had graduated at the head of his class from Virginia Military Institute in 1852.

The Lynchburg Rifles was outfitted locally. The *Lynchburg Daily Virginian* reported that the company was uniformed in "gray goods trimmed with blue," and existing photographs show that the men wore battle shirts into service. They also had locally made equipment and were armed with Springfield muskets.

The 11th Virginia was quickly sent forward to join the Confederate army near Manassas, Virginia. During the battle of First Manassas, both Companies E and H were engaged with the enemy at Blackburn's Ford. It was here that Captain

Blankenship showed that schooling did not necessarily make effective leadership—when things got hot during the fight, he turned and ran. Following the battle, the men of the 11th Virginia scoured the field and equipped themselves with new weapons and all other needed accoutrements. By the end of July, the company was outfitted as well as any in the Southern army.

TIMOTHY OSTERHELD

CHARLESTON ZOUAVE CADETS

Southern militiamen were no more immune than their Northern brethren to the Zouave craze fostered by the tour of Elmer Ellsworth's U.S. Zouave Cadets in the summer of 1860. In Charleston, South Carolina, a notice in the *Daily Courier* called for the raising of a military company to be named the Charleston Zouave Cadets. By the middle of August, the first meeting of the organization established a constitution for the company, and in October, officers were elected.

Determining a uniform was not as easy, and in the end, although the original constitution had called for a dress uniform "similar to the full uniform of the French Zouaves," when the company paraded for the first time, the men wore gray fatigue jackets and pants with red trim, accented "with white crossbelts." This was not a Zouave uniform, and even when the company adopted a full dress, or winter, uniform in November, it too was gray.

This winter uniform was worn for the first time at a drill on December 14, 1861, six days before South Carolina announced its secession from the Union. Actually a modified French chasseur uniform, it featured a tight-fitting gray short coat with slits at the sides, again trimmed with red. White gaiters and leather greaves (leggings worn between knee and ankle) helped give their straight-legged gray trousers the appearance of Zouave trousers. Officers wore dark blue uniform coats and trousers trimmed with red facings and gilt lace. All members wore exceptionally natty red and blue forage caps, the officers' trimmed with gilt lace.

The Charleston Zouave Cadets had devised an attractive and efficient uniform, but it could not be accurately described as Zouave. The Zouave Cadets' main contribution to the war was guarding Union prisoners from the battle of Bull Run who were housed in Charleston's Castle Pinckney. There they wore their short fatigue jackets and trousers without gaiters or leather greaves. By February, the Zouave Cadets had disbanded, although some of the members went on to serve in an artillery company guarding Charleston Harbor.

DICK AND M. E. CLOW

An Austrian-style officer's forage cap (Lager Mutze) worn by Capt. Charles Burton of the 7th Connecticut Volunteers in the early part of the war. This style of cap, with a downward-pitched visor, was widely favored by both sides. Although christened a McDowell cap by modern collectors after the general who wore one, the evidence points to its origin in Europe as early as the 1850s or before. TROIANI COLLECTION.

An unusual enameled officer's belt, probably dating from before or very early in the war, with interlocking tongue-and-wreath Georgia buckle. The yellow coloring may indicate use by a cavalry officer. WILLIAM ERQUITT COLLECTION.

Typical of prewar firemen, this ornate belt and buckle are distinctively marked to the band of the 2nd Rhode Island Detached Militia. It was worn by musician William S. Dillway, who served about four months in late 1861. JOHN OCKERBLOOM COLLECTION.

White linen havelock worn by Sgt. Rollin B. Truesdell of Company F, 27th New York Volunteers. The regiment's historian commented: "On the march and in this battle [1st Bull Run] many men in the regiment wore white linen 'havelocks' with long capes over the back of the neck. These had been recommended to protect the wearers from the effect of the sun. The only good purpose they served, however was to furnish lint and bandages for the wounded, and were never worn much after this battle." TROIANI COLLECTION.

C. B. FAIRCHILD, *HISTORY OF THE 27TH REGIMENT N.Y. VOLUNTEERS* (BINGHAMTON, N.Y.: CARL MATTHEWS PRINTERS, 1888), 15.

Early-war Federal gray felt overcoat of substandard quality. Describing similar inferior overcoats, a reporter wrote in the December 19, 1861, Boston Evening Journal: "Holding the cloth up to the light, you can see the cheat; using a little strength, you feel it; it is like brown paper. The wind will blow through them as if they were sieves; the least strain tears them." This coat, in unused condition, still bears the contractor's paper size label on the front. TROIANI COLLECTION.

1st Minnesota Infantry, July 1861

The 1st Minnesota Infantry was raised in April 1861 from various small towns along the St. Croix and Minnesota Rivers. Most companies came together at Fort Snelling. The state made every effort to arm the proud, new regiment with the best weapons in its arsenal. Three companies received the M1855 rifle musket, while the rest were armed with a combination of M1841 rifles and smoothbore muskets altered from flint to percussion. Clothing was a more difficult problem. Only one company had uniforms, which had been made for the men by the women of their hometown. As luck would have, it the women had outfitted their soldiers in the color soon to be adopted by the enemy—gray. The remainder of the regiment received trousers and red woolen shirts purchased by the state from the stock of a St. Paul mercantile house. Several companies that had been temporarily stationed near Fort Ridgely, Minnesota, received old U.S. Army uniforms. Army forage caps were procured and issued in June, before the regiment left the state.

During May and June, the 1st Minnesota drilled and received a continual flow of visitors to their camp. On June 14, orders were received to move the regiment to Washington. As a parting gift, the men received 600 white cloth havelocks made for them by a local Ladies' Aid Society. These items, designed to fit over the army cap and extend down to cover the back of the neck, were touted as being indispensable to the soldiers' comfort. As the 1st Minnesota moved east, the Chicago press reported that the men in their red shirts were "looked upon as heroes of romance, frontiersmen and Indian fighters," according to the *St. Paul Pioneer and Democrat*.

DR. J. LINDSTROM

It was expected that when the regiment arrived in the East, it would be outfitted in the regulation uniform. But when the army finally moved across the Potomac to meet the Rebels, the men still wore the same basic dress they had on when they left home, including the red shirts that marked them as frontiersmen. They lost 160 of their number, killed and wounded, on the field of Bull Run. Soon after the battle, the entire regiment finally received its first issue of regulation army uniforms. It served the rest of the war in the common garb of the Union soldier, but the record of valor it gained in the hard-fighting II Corps was anything but common. The final record showed a total loss in combat of 10 officers and 177 enlisted men killed and mortally wounded.

6TH TEXAS INFANTRY, PRIVATES, COMPANY G, 1861–62

Throughout the Civil War, the state of Texas made every effort to take care of her sons serving in the Confederate army. This extended to all aspects of the soldiers' lives, be it arms, uniforms, or hospital care. This was particularly evident in 1861, but to the degree possible, it continued for the entire war.

Company G, 6th Texas Infantry, is an excellent example of the early state effort. The company was raised as the Travis Rifles in Austin during the summer of 1861. With patriotic fervor high, the people of Austin procured the material for tents and uniforms, and the ladies of the city used their sewing skill to make both. The first uniform was described as "a dark pepper and salt grey" and, as appropriate to a rifle company, it was trimmed in green. Like many early units, both Union and Confederate, despite its name, the company did not carry rifles. The original arms of the Travis Rifles were flintlock muskets that were rifled and altered to percussion ignition.

Despite the patriotic intentions, the uniforms manufactured for the Travis Rifles by the industrious women of Austin seem to have lasted for only a short time. The company moved from Austin to Camp McCulloch, Texas, where it became Company G of the new 6th Texas Infantry. While here, the entire regiment was outfitted in new uniforms made of a light brown material manufactured at the Texas State Penitentiary. They also received new smoothbore M1842 Springfield muskets, which fired a formidable buck and ball load, as well as new accoutrements, including belts and cartridge boxes. The regiment finally received rifles in early 1862, when several issues were made of M1841 Mississippi rifles.

DAVID RANKIN, JR.

The 6th Texas remained west of the Mississippi until early 1863, when it moved east to the Army of Tennessee. Here it was consolidated with the 10th Texas Infantry and the 15th Texas Dismounted Cavalry and, under Col. R. Q. Mill of the 10th, was assigned to Churchill's Brigade in the division commanded by the hard-fighting Irishman Patrick Cleburne.

62ND PENNSYLVANIA INFANTRY (33RD INDEPENDENT REGIMENT), 1861

The 62nd Pennsylvania Infantry was recruited in the counties of Allegheny, Clarion, Jefferson, and Blair in July 1861 by Col. Samuel W. Black as the 33rd Independent Regiment. The original numerical designation lasted only a short time, however, until a controversy was settled relating to the commissioning of officers. In early correspondence, the 62nd was most often referred to simply as Colonel Black's regiment, and it was by this designation that the initial uniform was supplied by the U.S. Quartermaster's Department. In early August, Colonel Black requested and received permission from Gen. George B. McClellan for his new regiment to be uniformed in the sky blue jackets of the style worn by the U.S. Army in the Mexican War. It serves as a testimony to both the efficiency and versatility of the Quartermaster's Department that it was able to quickly respond to this request, which was only one of hundreds received from the volunteer regiments being mustered for Federal service.

Within less than a month, the army had contracted with the firm of George W. Colladay in Philadelphia, and by August 31, the regiment received the initial delivery of the requested uniforms—247 pairs of sky blue trousers and 449 sky blue jackets. By early September, the regiment was uniformed and equipped and on its way to Washington. On the eleventh, it crossed the Potomac River into Virginia.

The sky blue uniforms of the 62nd served the regiment for less than six months. On January 22, 1862, Colonel Black's regiment, along with the 83rd Pennsylvania, was outfitted in the imported uniform of the French chasseur. It was in this dress that the regiment would see its first action—at Yorktown, Virginia, in April 1862. At Gaines' Mill on June 27, Colonel Black was killed in action.

By August 1862, the men of the 62nd no longer were distinguished by the uniform they wore. As they marched

PRIVATE COLLECTION

with the V Army Corps, they wore the standard uniform of the Federal soldier. But as one of the finest regiments in the Army of the Potomac, the 62nd needed only its record in battle to set it apart from the rest.

19th Alabama Infantry, Spring 1862

Early in June 1861, the Confederate secretary of war received a letter from Blount County, Alabama, offering the services of two companies that were "organized and . . . uniformed, drilled and ready to march." These companies, the Blount Continentals and the Blount Guards, were indeed ready to march, in uniforms with jackets cut much like a formal tailcoat. Although they surely felt every inch the warrior, the Continentals and Guards lacked one important ingredient: Like many of the brave young Southern men who were rallying to the colors of the new nation, the men of Blount County had no weapons.

By August, these companies had joined others from Pickens, Jefferson, and Cherokee Counties in camp near Huntsville and had been mustered as Companies B and K of the 19th Alabama Infantry. The lack of arms had required the new regiment to enlist for the period of the war, while others who came with their own weapons were allowed to enlist for twelve months' service. While at Huntsville, the new regiment was outfitted with all the necessities of a soldier's life. Camp kettles, tents, mess pans, axes, and spades were supplied, and each man received a tin cup and plate, but although these items prepared them for service, they would hardly strike fear in the heart of any Yankee.

It was not until January 1862, while in camp near Pensacola, Florida, that the 19th Alabama received the weapons they would carry into battle. Photographic evidence shows that at least some of the arms received were M1841 Mississippi rifles sporting an intimidating and unique bayonet, which could also serve effectively as a sword. Here at last were the tools that would allow the regiment to show what it

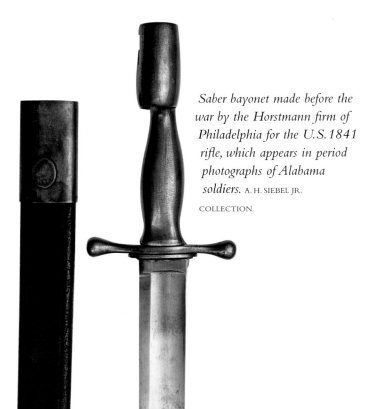

Saber bayonet made before the war by the Horstmann firm of Philadelphia for the U.S. 1841 rifle, which appears in period photographs of Alabama soldiers. A. H. SIEBEL JR. COLLECTION.

DICK AND M. E. CLOW

could do. And it did not have long to wait. On April 6, as part of Gen. Albert Sidney Johnston's Army of the Mississippi, the 19th Alabama was part of the surprise dawn attack on the Union army camped around Shiloh Church, near Pittsburg Landing, Tennessee. During the heavy two-day fighting, the Alabamians suffered 219 killed and wounded, a casualty list that amounted to one-third of the number engaged.

2ND NEW HAMPSHIRE VOLUNTEERS, 1861

Although New Hampshire was asked for only one regiment of infantry with Lincoln's call for 75,000 volunteers in April 1861, so many responded that a second regiment was also formed from the eager volunteers. Four of its companies had been prewar militia companies, and the choice of gray for the regiment's initial uniform may have reflected this heritage. Wearing a "spike-tail" coatee with red trim, gray trousers striped with red, and "jaunty forage caps" of gray with red bands, the 2nd New Hampshire carried M1842 buck and ball muskets. One company carried Sharps breech-loading rifles provided by subscriptions of the citizens of Concord. Soon after Bull Run, the muskets were replaced with rifle muskets.

In fact, the regiment was fully equipped when it left the state for Washington in the spring of 1861. Each soldier was issued a "grey coat and pants, grey overcoat, grey fatigue cap, two flannel shirts, one pair of flannel drawers, one extra pair of socks, one pair of shoes, and one large camp blanket." He also received an "india rubber knapsack" with his accoutrements. By June, the *Washington, D.C., Evening Star* reported that the regiment's uniform included "grey caps and pants and blue jackets."

The 2nd fought at First Bull Run in its gray uniforms, but it wore Federal blue thereafter as it fought with the Army of the Potomac in every important battle to 1865.

COLLECTION OF KELLY OSMER

Large (12-by-12-inch) unpainted canvas haversack of the pattern issued to early volunteer regiments from New Hampshire. This example was used by Sgt. Nathan T. Brown of the 6th New Hampshire Volunteers. Note the unusual double-button arrangement to secure the flap. TROIANI COLLECTION.

Commercially manufactured forage cap provided to at least the first sixteen regiments from New Hampshire. Of a quality more often associated with officers, these caps were dressed with the silvered letters "NHV," in addition to a false embroidered hunting horn in brass or silver finish, with regimental and company designations. Some examples of this cap have horns of gilt brass despite the silver color of the other insignia. TROIANI COLLECTION.

Sumter Light Guard, Company K, 4th Georgia Infantry, April 1861

The Sumter Light Guard was one of numerous Georgia companies mustered into Confederate service wearing a uniform of its own design. In late April 1861, the *Augusta Chronicle and Sentinel* described the regiment: "This splendid corps arrived in town on Sunday morning. They number 83 men. They were accompanied by the American Brass Band, whose performance elicited general approval and eulogy from our citizens. They only escort the corps thus far on their journey. The Uniform of the Sumter Light Guards is a dark blue jacket, for the privates, trimmed with buff."

Within a matter of days, the Sumter Light Guard was mustered into Confederate service as Company K, 4th Georgia Infantry. The 4th Georgia was initially armed with smoothbore muskets, which were probably some of those purchased by the state in the North prior to the outbreak of the war. The regiment became part of the II Corps of the Army of Northern Virginia, and its history is interwoven with that famed army and corps.

A prewar stamped brass Georgia state seal hat device. Examples are known with both a gilt and silver finish and have been excavated on Civil War sites near Savannah and in South Carolina. William Erquitt collection.

Pvt. Milton J. Wolf of Company L, 28th Pennsylvania Volunteers, wore this short gray uniform jacket. Although the state of Pennsylvania contracted for a large number of cadet gray uniforms in early 1861, Col. John W. Geary chose to uniform and equip the 28th out of his own pocketbook. These garments were most likely replaced by the regulation blue before the beginning of the 1862 campaigns. COURTESY OF PAMPLIN HISTORICAL PARK AND THE NATIONAL MUSEUM OF THE CIVIL WAR SOLDIER.

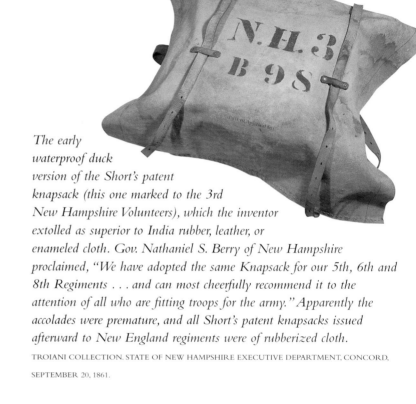

The early waterproof duck version of the Short's patent knapsack (this one marked to the 3rd New Hampshire Volunteers), which the inventor extolled as superior to India rubber, leather, or enameled cloth. Gov. Nathaniel S. Berry of New Hampshire proclaimed, "We have adopted the same Knapsack for our 5th, 6th and 8th Regiments . . . and can most cheerfully recommend it to the attention of all who are fitting troops for the army." Apparently the accolades were premature, and all Short's patent knapsacks issued afterward to New England regiments were of rubberized cloth. TROIANI COLLECTION. STATE OF NEW HAMPSHIRE EXECUTIVE DEPARTMENT, CONCORD, SEPTEMBER 20, 1861.

This whimsical camp or smoking cap was probably handmade by Pvt. Charles L. Comes of the 8th Louisiana Infantry. Such headwear was popular during idle hours in camp, which constituted much of a soldier's service. Comes was killed in action on the first day at Gettysburg. CONFEDERATE MEMORIAL HALL, CLAUDE LEVET PHOTOGRAPH.

Undoubtedly the most curious headgear donned in the war was the Whipple's patent cap. Patented in July 1861 by J. F. Whipple, it was produced by the Seamless Clothing Manufacturing Company and initially proved popular, especially among New England units, until the rigors of campaigning condemned it to an early extinction. There appear to have been two varieties: the solid-body felt type (shown) and a two-piece construction of a treated soft material with a center seam in the crown. The intensely bright blue cap shown here is one of the few surviving examples. TROIANI COLLECTION.

17TH MISSISSIPPI INFANTRY, COMPANY I, PETTUS RIFLES

The 17th Mississippi Infantry was mustered into Confederate service on June 1, 1861, to serve for a period of twelve months. Among those sworn to serve the new nation were the men of Company I, the Pettus Rifles, commanded by Capt. Marmaduke Bell, who had organized the company at Cockrums, De Soto County. The regiment left the state on June 13, headed for Virginia. Ahead of it lay four years of war in the ranks of the Army of Northern Virginia.

When they left Mississippi, the men of Captain Bell's company wore a uniform that, as closely as any, represented that prescribed prior to the war by the state for her troops. For reasons that may have reflected the desire for the predominance of states rights, Mississippi had decided to assign the infantry of her state army the trim color traditionally reserved for artillery—red. The company had been armed with muskets and bayonets, complete sets of accoutrements, canteens, and knapsacks. Whereas most of the uniforms were locally manufactured, the state quartermaster had supplied the buttons, described in requisitions simply as "Infantry buttons."

As with most early state-issue uniforms, that of the Pettus Rifles was replaced soon after actual campaigning had begun. By early 1862, the uniforms of the 17th were replaced by more standard Confederate issue, which the regiment wore for the remainder of the war. The original knapsacks continued in service at least until the end of 1861. The file of a private of Company C who was killed in action at the battle of Leesburg on October 21, 1861, states that because his knapsack was "thrown away on entering the fight and not found," he had no private effects to send home. It took over a year of campaigning before the soldiers of both armies learned that discarding or stacking of knapsacks before a battle usually resulted in their loss.

DICK AND M. E. CLOW

Confederate copy of a U.S. model 1845 percussion cap pouch made in Columbus, Mississippi, during the early days of the war. The finial was often made of lead instead of brass. NELSONIAN INSTITUTE.

THE STANLY MARKSMEN, COMPANY H, 14TH NORTH CAROLINA INFANTRY

The Civil War had begun. Confederate forces, in Charleston Harbor, fired upon Fort Sumter and Pres. Abraham Lincoln issued a call for 75,000 men to put down the Rebellion. In an article in the *Stanly (North Carolina) News and Press* Dr. Richard Anderson of Abemarle, Stanly County, asked of his fellow townspeople, "What was Stanly County to do?" Their own governor, John W. Ellis, wanted to recruit 10,000 volunteers to help defend Virginia. The majority of the populace of Stanly County were farmers; few owned slaves. Caring little for politics, they wanted to live and work their farms in peace. Dr. Anderson's question received no response. The crowd that had gathered in the second-story courtroom at the Abemarle Courthouse remained passively quiet. Anderson slowly rose from his chair and said, "I'm ask-

ing for volunteers to make up a company for Stanly County." The crowd now grew restless. Anderson's call for volunteers was passed from person to person, down the stairs to the first floor and out to those who gathered on the courthouse steps. One young man, Robert Carter, was told of the request for volunteers to support the secessionists. "Well, I'll go! I'll GO!" he shouted. Young Carter began pushing his way up to the second floor. All turned to look, then another young voice called out, "I'll go too! I'll volunteer!" Stanly County thus raised a company of 104 men to fight for the new Confederacy.

In the days that followed, the city of Abemarle dedicated itself to the care of the Stanly Marksmen. Young ladies tied ribbons around the arms of each new volunteer. A Committee was formed of concerned citizens to help clothe and equip the men for active service. The minute book of the committee states that gray cloth was procured for uniforms—darker gray for the coats, lighter gray for the trousers. A red grosgrain ribbon was used for the facings. The county's first sewing machine was pressed into service, as two local tailors, John Williams and Tommy Haskell, worked night and day sewing the garments. The ladies, supervised by "Aunt Tempe" Russell, cut up the cloth to pattern for the tailors.

The uniform dress of the Stanly County Marksmen was a frock coat with a high collar, "a chest full of red braid," and light gray trousers. The committee also supplied the company with twelve water buckets, seven club axes, seven hatchets, fourteen tents, thirty frying pans, ninety tin plates, and hats and shoes for all.

On May 5, 1861, they were sworn into state service as Company H, 4th North Carolina Volunteers. They later became Company H, 14th North Carolina Infantry, fighting in all the major battles of the Army of Northern Virginia. Four long years later, only 9 of the original 104 men surrendered at Appomattox Courthouse.

The history of how the Stanly County Marksmen procured their first uniforms is atypical of most early Confederate companies. Theirs were donated uniforms, made locally. Most other Confederate companies received uniforms from their home state, purchased them from private contractors, or marched to their assembly camps in their civilian clothes, hoping to buy or receive new clothing there. The new Confederate government allotted $21 to each new volunteer to spend on military clothing. But by the late summer of 1861, all the martial finery was gone. Warm winter clothing, wool socks, blankets, flannel shirts, wool overcoats, jackets, shoes, and boots were sent out to the armies. Now parades and fancy uniforms were just a fond memory for the Stanly County Marksmen.

Dark blue satinette frock coat worn by John Crozier of Company E, 1st Delaware Volunteers, during his three months of service in early 1861. The coat is of simple construction, the only ornamentation being a light blue tape edging around the collar. There is a gap in the spacing of the buttons where the waist belt plate would have rested. The uniforms of Company D of this regiment (and possibly others) were made by the patriotic ladies of St. Paul's M.E. Church. (DELAWARE GAZETTE, MAY 14, 1861.) TROIANI COLLECTION.

Right: *The state of New Hampshire furnished austere frock coats of its own pattern to the first eight regiments from that state. Fully lined, they were made of a shoddy material, without ornamentation of any sort except a light blue cord edging to the shoulder straps that lay under the brass shoulder scales. This example was worn in 1862 by John Currier, a forty-eight-year-old musician of the 6th New Hampshire Volunteers.* TROIANI COLLECTION.

MILITIA AND EARLY VOLUNTEERS

INTRODUCTION

1. Robert Weir, *Regulations for the Uniforms and Dress of the Army of the United States* (Boston: Robert Weir Publishers, 1857), 83.
2. Frederick P. Todd, *American Military Equipage, 1851–1872*, vols. 1 and 2 (n.p.: Chatham Square, 1983).
3. *Military Gazette,* December 1860, p. 353.
4. Michael J. Winey, "Pennsylvanians in Gray," *Military Images* (July–August 1982), 92.
5. National Archives, Record Group 109, M-437, Letters Received by the Confederate Secretary of War.

6TH REGIMENT, MASSACHUSETTS VOLUNTEER MILITIA, 1861

Charles W. Hall, *Regiments and Armories of Massachusetts* (Boston: W. W. Potter, 1899).

The Massachusetts Register, (Boston: Adams, Sampson, 1862).
Washington, D.C., Evening Star, April 20, 1861, 3.

PRIVATE, MARYLAND GUARD, 1861

Baltimore American and Commercial Advertiser, January 16, 1860.
Reflections and Opinions of James McHenry Howard (Baltimore: Wm. Wilkins, 1903), 27.

7TH REGIMENT, NEW YORK STATE MILITIA, 8TH COMPANY, 1861

Emmons Clark, *History of the Seventh Regiment of New York,* (New York: The Seventh Regiment, 1890).
Washington, D.C., Evening Star, April 25, 1861, 2.

1ST REGIMENT SOUTH CAROLINA RIFLES, 1861

National Archives, M-267, Compiled Service Records of Confederate Soldiers, South Carolina, December 17, 1862.

DRIVE THEM TO WASHINGTON

National Archives, Record Group 109, M-468, Compiled Service Records of Soldiers Who Served in Organizations from the State of Virginia, 4th Virginia Infantry.

PRIVATE, COMPANY I, 4TH VIRGINIA INFANTRY C.S.A., THE LIBERTY HALL VOLUNTEERS

National Archives, Record Group 109, M-324, Compiled Service Records of Confederate Soldiers Who Served from Virginia, 4th Virginia Infantry.

FLAT RIVER GUARD, COMPANY B, 6TH NORTH CAROLINA STATE TROOPS INFANTRY

Frederick P. Todd, *American Military Equipage, 1851–1872,* vol. 2 (n.p.: Chatham Square, 1983).
Richard W. Iobst, *The Bloody Sixth* (Raleigh: North Carolina Centennial Commission, 1965), 5.

CLINCH RIFLES, GEORGIA MILITIA, APRIL 1861

Augusta Daily Constitution, October 14, 1860.
Original Orderly Book, Clinch Rifles, July 18, 1860.
Augusta Chronicle and Sentinel, May 7, 1861.

THE FIRST BATTLE FLAGS

Letter written by Lt. Colin McRae Selph, July 25, 1905, Louisiana Historical Association Papers, Tulane University Library.

3RD ALABAMA INFANTRY, COMPANY A, MOBILE CADETS, 1861

William. S. Coker, ed., *The Mobile Cadets, 1845–1945: A Century of Honor and Fidelity* (Bagdad, Fla.: Patagonia Press, 1993), 19, 29.

Frederick P. Todd, *American Military Equipage,* 1851–1872, vol. 2 (n.p.: Chatham Square, 1983).

National Archives, Record Group 109, M-331, Compiled Service Records of Confederate General and Staff Officers and Nonregimental Enlisted Men, roll 265, Lt. Col. James L. White.

www.rootsweb.com, 3rd Alabama History.

1ST RHODE ISLAND DETACHED MILITIA, 1861

Augustus Woodbury, *A Narrative of the Campaign* (Providence: Sidney S. Rider, 1862).

Original Uniform of Edward N. Whittier, 1st Rhode Island Detached Militia, Don Troiani Collection.

11TH VIRGINIA INFANTRY, COMPANY E, THE LYNCHBURG RIFLES, JULY 1861

National Archives, Record Group 109, M-324, Compiled Service Records of Confederate Soldiers Who Served in Organizations from Virginia, 11th Virginia Infantry.

Lynchburg Daily Virginian, May 1, 1861.

Rusty Hicks and Adam Scher, "Piedmont Battle Shirts," *Military Images* (November–December 1995): 9–14.

Robert T. Bell, *11th Virginia Infantry* (Lynchburg, Va.: H. E. Howard, 1985), 11.

CHARLESTON ZOUAVE CADETS

Charleston Daily Courier, July 30, 1860.

Frederick P. Todd, "Notes on the Organization and Uniforms of South Carolina Military Forces," *Military Collector and Historian* 3, no. 3 (September 1951): 53–62.

Ron Field, "Charleston Tigers," *Military Illustrated* no. 103 (December 1996).

1ST MINNESOTA INFANTRY, JULY 1861

Annual Report of the Adjutant General of Minnesota, St. Paul, 1861.

Quote from a Chicago paper of June 28, 1861, found in the June 29 *St. Paul Pioneer and Democrat.*

Todd H. Fredericks and Stephen E. Osman, "Minnesota 1st Volunteer Infantry, 1861–1864," *Military Collector and Historian* 47, no. 2 (summer 1995): 83–89.

Frederick H. Dyer, *A Compendium of the War of the Rebellion* (New York: Thomas Yoseloff, 1959).

6TH TEXAS INFANTRY, PRIVATES, COMPANY G, 1861–62

Jim Turner, "Co. G, 6th Texas Infantry, C.S.A., from 1861 to 1865," *Texana* 12, no. 2 (spring 1974): 149–78.

Richard A. Baumgartner and Larry M. Strayer, *Echoes of Battle* (Huntington, W.V.: Blue Acorn Press, 1996).

National Archives, Record Group 109, Personnel Files of the 6th Texas Infantry.

62ND PENNSYLVANIA INFANTRY (33RD INDEPENDENT REGIMENT), 1861

National Archives, Record Group 92, entry 2194, book 3; and Record Group 94, Regimental Books, 62nd Pennsylvania Infantry.

19TH ALABAMA INFANTRY, SPRING 1862

National Archives, Record Group 109, M-437, Letters Received by the Confederate Secretary of War; and M-374, Compiled Service Records of Confederate Soldiers Who Served from Alabama, 19th Infantry.

John M. Murphy and Howard Michael Madaus, *Confederate Rifles and Muskets* (Newport Beach, Calif.: Graphic Publishers, 1996), 503.

War of the Rebellion: A Compilation of the Official Records of the Union and Confederate Armies, vol. 20 (Washington, D.C.: Government Printing Office, 1901).

2ND NEW HAMPSHIRE VOLUNTEERS, 1861

Martin A. Haynes, *A History of the Second New Hampshire Volunteer Infantry* (Lakeport, N.H., 1896).

Washington, D.C., Evening Star, June 24, 1861, 3.

SUMTER LIGHT GUARD, COMPANY K, 4TH GEORGIA INFANTRY, APRIL 1861

Augusta Chronicle and Sentinel, April 30, 1861.

National Archives, Record Group 109, M-266, Compiled Service Records of Confederate Soldiers Who Served in Organizations from the State of Georgia.

Frederick P. Todd, *American Military Equipage,* 1851–1872, vol. 2 (n.p.: Chatham Square, 1983).

17TH MISSISSIPPI INFANTRY, COMPANY I, PETTUS RIFLES

National Archives Record Group 109, M-269, Compiled Service Records of Confederate Soldiers Who Served in Organizations from the State of Mississippi, Records of the 17th Mississippi.

THE STANLY MARKSMEN, COMPANY H, 14TH NORTH CAROLINA INFANTRY

"First Stanly Civil War Unit Was Heroic, Colorful Group," *Stanly (North Carolina) News and Press,* October 10, 1962.

Volunteers of Many Nations

THE AMERICAN NATION IN 1861 WAS BEGINNING to reflect the diversity of population that would characterize our national experience into the twentieth century. During the seventeenth and eighteenth centuries, the colonies that became the United States were composed mainly of people of English descent. A few Dutch, French Huguenot, German, and Scots-Irish immigrants were interspersed in this relatively homogeneous population and added to the vitality of the new nation. In the years before the Civil War began, however, a major wave of immigration hit the American shores, changing forever the national character and contributing to the diversity of the military uniforms worn by the Civil War soldiers.

From the 1820s through the 1850s, the numbers of these new immigrants reached levels never before seen. In the 1820s, immigration numbered around 10,000 persons a year. In 1854 alone, over 420,000 new immigrants arrived in the United States. Although these numbers would be dwarfed by the millions of immigrants who arrived in the twentieth century, they were sufficient to cause a backlash against immigration from the native-born and descendants of earlier immigrants. The Know-Nothing movement of the 1850s was a hypocritical attempt to ensure that these new Americans would not "corrupt" the values of a political system already terminally divided over the issue of slavery. It was reflected even in the militia system. New Irish immigrants formed a regiment, the 69th New York State Militia, whose ultimate purpose was the liberation of Ireland. German immigrants gathered in units such as the 5th New York State Militia to practice target shooting and celebrate the liberties found in their new home, while some native-born reacted by forming strictly "American" organizations such as the 71st New York State Militia, known as the American Guard. Each

was in its own way a reflection of the national origin of its members, but the regiments also reflected the nation itself as they came together in 1861 for the war.

Since the waves of nineteenth-century immigrants tended to settle in the Northeast and Western states, most of the foreign-born volunteers served in the Northern armies. Only the more cosmopolitan cities of the South, such as Charleston, South Carolina, and New Orleans, had sufficient numbers of foreign-born to form distinctive units. In Charleston, before the war, among the militia companies at the start of the war were the German Artillery, complete with spiked helmets known as *Pickelhaubes;* the Union Light Infantry, in Scottish trews; the Lafayette Artillery, in French frock coats and red trousers; and the Montgomery Guard, in traditional Irish green coatees. In New Orleans, in 1860, the Creole Zouaves were described as wearing chasseur uniforms, including a "coat of navy blue, with gilt buttons, skirts only five or six inches deep," and "Turkish trousers of light blue, full and baggy." These national uniforms would soon disappear in the South, as the Confederate military ran into insurmountable problems of procurement and distribution. Confederate clothing manufactories were not so flexible as their Northern counterparts, and distinctive uniforms of any sort tended to disappear in the Southern forces. Irishmen, Germans, and Scots who served with the South soon lost their national flavor.[1]

In the North, the militia companies and regiments also often reflected the national origin of their members. Thus Scotsmen in kilts could be found equally in New York or Illinois, and French Zouaves and chasseurs, or at least their uniforms, ranged from Missouri to Massachusetts. Germans in spiked helmets were not found solely in Charleston, as *Pickelhaubes* appear in advertisements throughout the Northern papers. Still, despite the better resources of Northern quarter-masters, there were few truly national uniforms worn by even Federal volunteers as the war progressed.

Whereas Zouave and chasseur uniforms were common throughout the war, there were few true Frenchmen wearing them. The old 55th Regiment of the New York State Militia—in existence since the 1840s as a company of French-Americans—was hard-pressed to fill its ranks with volunteers of French ancestry; nevertheless, its infantry went to war in a version of the French campaign uniform, and its Zouaves were as splendidly attired as any North African regiment. A few French veterans found their way into the 62nd New York, the Anderson Zouaves, whose flank companies also wore a full-rigged Zouave uniform, but for the most part there was more influence than service from French immigrants, whose actual numbers were few in wartime America.

The much more numerous German population often had a Teutonic flair in the manner in which it wore its uniforms, but there were relatively few volunteer regiments in German dress. When the early Ohio volunteers from Cincinnati departed for war, members of the 9th Ohio wore the white clothing of the Turner Societies—social and athletic clubs organized in a quasimilitary fashion—and some even took their target rifles with vicious-looking knife bayonets to war. The 41st New York went to war in green and red uniforms based upon the traditional garb of Prussian Rifle regiments. They did, however, somewhat spoil the effect with the addition of a French Zouave company to the regiment. The German riflemen of the 20th New York Volunteer Infantry wore Federal blue but did sport the traditional German marksman lanyard, or aiguillette, from the front of their coats. Louis Blenker's 1st German Rifles wore a simple gray and green uniform that had less German styling than practicality. Although the overall contribution of the German-American population to the war was tremendous, for the most part German volunteers blended into the mainstream.

Although often mentioned and completely romanticized, the use of Scots Highlander uniforms appears to have been limited to the original members of the 79th New York State Militia, who served with the 79th Volunteer Regiment during the war. The prewar kilts were worn by those former militiamen who had them when the regiment left New York City, but trews, trousers of tartan cloth, were worn afterward until replaced by Federal blue. The only distinctly Scots garments to see sustained service were caps of either the glengarry or tam-o'-shanter styles, worn by the 79th and other predominantly Scots units such as the 12th Illinois.

Another national uniform used during the war was the *bersaglieri,* or Italian light infantry, uniform mimicked by the 39th New York, the Garibaldi Guard. The men of the 39th New York, however, were not all of Italian descent, and even the regiment's colonel, Frederic George D'Utassy, was not Italian. In fact, D'Utassy's regiment was one of the most cosmopolitan of all the volunteer regiments. It was reported that the regiment included "three companies each of German and Hungarians and one company each of Frenchmen, Italians, Spaniards and Swiss."[2] The loose, red "Garibaldi shirt," patterned after those worn by the original Italian national patriots of Garibaldi's army, was, however, a frequently mentioned garb of early war volunteers.

Perhaps most surprising is the lack of any distinctly Irish garb among the volunteers. The Irish-American population was quite sizable during the American Civil War and was second only to the number of German-Americans in the Union armies. Irish-Americans, however, did not go to war in green uniforms like those worn earlier in the century by Irish militia companies. Instead, except for Thomas F. Meagher's green general's uniform and a reported green vest in the Irish Brigade, most Irishmen went to war in the issued uniform of a state or the Federal government. Even the Irishmen of New York's 69th State Militia Regiment had given up their green uniforms for regulation blue years before the war began.[3] Still, the Irish green battle flags of regiments from several states dotted many a Civil War battlefield.

Foreign volunteers fought and died, North and South alike. Their contributions to our history are invaluable, and even though most of the volunteers of the war—fully three-quarters of the Union army—were native born, the very real color their few distinctive uniforms added to the war only highlights their story.

Irish Jasper Greens, Lance Corporal, Fall 1861

On August 24, 1861, with all the eloquence of nineteenth-century oratory, the Irish Jasper Greens of Savannah were presented with a new flag. The flag was a gift from several young ladies of the city and symbolized both allegiance to the state and the ethnic makeup of the organization. One side was of white silk, with the coat of arms of Georgia surmounted by eleven gold stars, and the reverse side was of green silk, upon which was embroidered the Harp of Erin along with the name of the company and the date of its organization, 1842. At the time of presentation, the Greens numbered about 100 men, commanded by Capt. John Foley. A detachment of the company had been ordered to garrison Fort Pulaski in January, and now the entire unit was preparing to move to augment the garrison of the fort.

Militia units such as the Irish Jasper Greens were very much a part of the fabric of prewar Savannah. The rules and minutes meticulously kept by the Greens leave no doubt that these sons of Erin were among the best. In 1861, the company had both a fatigue and a dress uniform, both of dark blue trimmed in green. It was the fatigue uniform that the men wore to duty at Fort Pulaski. In the organization's rules, it is described as "a blue jacket with green collar and cuffs, 10 buttons in front, straps on the shoulders to pass the belts under." The trousers for both uniforms were the same but were dependent upon the season—for summer, white linen with no stripe, and for cooler weather, dark blue with a 1½-inch green stripe edged with buff down the outer seam. Rank was indicated by chevrons of "green army lace on green cloth laced with buff showing green between the chevrons . . . pointing upwards." The rank of lance corporal, indicated by a single chevron, placed its wearer in a command structure between a private and a full corporal. No description of the headgear of the company is recorded, but several references are made to white plumes, which would have been used with the shako popular at the time. The meeting minutes of April 19, 1860, show that

DR. COYLE S. CONNOLLY

the company also purchased fatigue caps. Given the meticulous care invested in the design of the rest of the uniform, these caps most certainly were designed to complement the rest of the fatigue dress. The property returns of the Irish Jasper Greens for December 1861 indicate that while the muskets carried by the company belonged to the state of Georgia, most accoutrements worn to war were the property of the Confederate States. Of plain leather, these replaced the white buff belts worn prior to the war.

COMPANY K, 69TH NEW YORK STATE MILITIA

Irish-Americans in New York City had formed militia companies since the eighteenth century, but the most Irish of all militia regiments, the 69th New York, was not organized until October 1851. It was formed from eight existing militia companies and confirmed by General Order No. 489 on November 1, 1851. The 69th is a part of New York's military heritage to this day, and its name became legendary during the Civil War, beginning at the battle of First Bull Run.

The colonel of the 69th, Michael Corcoran, gathered many Irish volunteers to bring the militia regiment to war strength, including a new Company K to replace the troop of cavalry in the militia organization. The new company, known as the Irish Zouaves, was recruited by Thomas Francis Meagher. Meagher, in exile from his native Ireland, was a political activist and Irish-American politician, and a major force in attracting volunteers. His men did not wear full Zouave uniforms, retaining only the short, open jacket and vest of the French originals. Meagher and the other officers of the Irish Zouaves wore similar uniforms, with gold braid on their jackets and crimson and gold stripes on their pants. Their weapons were M1816 muskets altered to the Maynard primer system and rifled, while the rest of the regiment carried M1842 muskets.

The 69th lost nearly 200 men at Bull Run as casualties and prisoners. Corcoran was captured and taken to Richmond as a prisoner. Meagher was wounded and carried from the field while unconscious. His Zouaves fought bravely, one of them saving the regimental color from capture at the end of the battle. The battered regiment returned to New York City, where a new volunteer 69th was raised. It became the core of the famed Irish Brigade, commanded by Gen. Thomas Francis Meagher.

WILLIAM RODEN

This model 1858 U.S. canteen with blue woolen cover belonged to Pvt. Daniel O'Hare of Company B, 69th New York State Volunteers. O'Hare joined on September 21, 1861, and deserted the same day, taking his newly issued canteen with him. TROIANI COLLECTION.

8TH AND 20TH NEW YORK VOLUNTEER INFANTRY, 1861

The large German-American population of the North was among the first to rally to the defense of the Union in 1861. In all, over 200,000 of these immigrant Americans would enlist in the Federal armies. Some of them were not only eager volunteers, but distinctly dressed as well. Two New York City German regiments, the 8th and 20th Volunteer Infantry, wore uniforms reflecting the Germanic tradition of marksmanship and the use of rifles.

The 8th, calling itself the 1st German Rifles and commanded by Louis (Ludwig) Blenker, was actually issued M1842 muskets rather than rifles, but still placed the distinctive green trim of a rifle unit on their gray uniforms. Uniformed in a gray sack with a strap and buckle behind, gray pantaloons with a broad green stripe down the side, and a gray cap with green cord, the 1st German Rifles was only one of several Union regiments in gray in 1861. More distinctive was the regimental engineer corps—the Pioneers, a splendid body of handicrafters, all equipped with India rubber aprons, axes, hatchets, knives, and other paraphernalia. These men led the regiment into Virginia in July 1861, where they served in the reserves at First Bull Run, though they did help turn back Confederate cavalry in the rearguard action of the Union retreat.

The 20th, called the United Turner Rifles, was issued and continued to carry throughout its service the M1841 rifle, also popularly called the jaeger or Mississippi rifle. This was truly a regiment of riflemen from its inception, having received 720 U.S. rifles with saber bayonets and 240 with socket bayonets fitted by an Albany, New York, mechanic named Frederick H. Grosz upon muster from the state of New York.

The United Turner Rifles, named after the Turnverein, German athletic societies that also fostered the use of firearms for marksmanship, also wore a distinctive uniform. Their dark blue frock coats had shoulder straps and were trimmed with a Germanic marksman lanyard, or aiguillette, worn looped from the shoulder. Their Federal-style uniform or Hardee hats were trimmed with rifle insignia, and all trim, including the hat cords, was in rifle green. At Antietam, with their Swedish colonel, Ernst von Vegasack, the 20th stormed across the open fields between the East and the West Woods to the Dunker Church, their regimental colors in the front, Vegasack crying of the colors, "Let them wave. They are our Glory!"

PRIVATE COLLECTION

Officer's metal-backed hat insignia of the 8th New York Volunteers, with an embroidered trumpet and silver number 8 on a dark green velvet ground.

TROIANI COLLECTION.

79TH NEW YORK HIGHLANDERS, 1861

Most militia regiments that served in the American Civil War limited their service to thirty to ninety days, the legal limits set on required participation. Some units were so eager to go war in 1861 that they forfeited their militia status to serve longer periods. The 79th New York State Militia was such a regiment. It was added to New York's militia rosters in 1859, but only after some controversy, as state authorities were not eager to add another regiment of immigrants into a system they sought to regiment by eliminating distinctiveness. Indeed, the regiment's required bill of dress stipulated that only trousers be worn, although they could be of plaid cloth. If the state had its way, the new regiment, which was allowed to take the regimental number 79 in honor of Great Britain's regiment of Cameron Highlanders, even though it was out of sequence, would have been just another militia regiment.

The Scotsmen of the 79th, however, were not to be just another regiment. This became clear at the regiment's first parade, when the men marched in Manhattan wearing not pants, but kilts. Though these Scots wearing "short petticoats and bare knees" were described as being "in poor taste and barbarous," the 79th persisted, and the men thereafter wore their kilts in every parade until the war came in 1861. To go to war, the regiment had to nearly double its size with recruits, but it was impossible to obtain sufficient material for kilts for the new members. Another result of getting these recruits was that enough

DICK AND M. E. CLOW

other militia units had already gone to war to fill the state's quota. If the 79th were to go to war, it would have to go as a Federal volunteer regiment, which it willingly agreed to do in order to fight.

On June 2, 1861, the 79th went to war, with the screech of bagpipes and here and there the bare knees of men in kilts. The original militia members of the 79th wore their kilts in this parade, with the officers in the colors of their clans. The new men wore plaid trousers, with the cutaway kilt jackets of

the regiment, trimmed with red and white. Armed with converted flintlock muskets, it was still obviously an ethnic regiment, but more importantly, it was a regiment with pride that would carry it through three years of war. From First Bull Run, where the 79th lost its colonel, James Cameron, the brother of Lincoln's secretary of war Simon Cameron, to such far-flung actions as Secessionville in South Carolina, Antietam, Vicksburg, Knoxville, the Wilderness, and Spotsylvania, the Scotsmen of the 79th were true to their regiment.

12TH ILLINOIS INFANTRY, 1ST SCOTTISH REGIMENT

Like many of the early Union volunteers, the 12th Illinois Infantry, originally known as the 1st Scottish Regiment, left for war dressed in gray. This regiment was raised in different parts of the state, and for the first months of service, its men wore a variety of dress that reflected the tastes of the individual counties and towns, as well as their ability to clothe their sons for battle. By August 1861, the need to enlist soldiers for more than a few months' service prompted the state of Illinois to offer a fine, new gray uniform for the first six regiments, now designated as the 7th through 12th Illinois Volunteers. The coat was to have a short skirt extending midway to the knee and be trimmed in light blue. In addition, the men would receive a fatigue uniform consisting of a shirt and pantaloons of fine hickory cloth and a Zouave cap. A hat of gray felt was also included with the dress uniform, but contemporary photographs of men of the 12th show them in Scottish tams, which were worn to honor their first colonel, John McArthur of Chicago. Although the uniform itself was consistent within the various regiments, Regimental Special Order No. 21 was issued at Paducah, Kentucky, on October 9, 1861, to address the fact that sergeants and corporals of the 12th were wearing chevrons of differing colors. The order specified that all chevrons and trouser stripes would in the future be of light blue worsted wool or cloth. It also established chevrons of three stripes and a single tie for company quartermaster and commissary sergeants.

On September 23, 1861, a War Department order mandated that all regiments in U.S. service discontinue wearing gray, the color adopted by the enemy. It was not until March of the following year, however, that the regiment received blue replacement uniforms.

The early muster rolls of the various companies refer to the arms of the regiment simply as "old Muskets," which is consistent with those issued to nearly all of the early Illinois regiments. By the fall of 1862, the Federal government had gotten the arms situation in hand with a combination of

imported and domestic firearms. The 12th would be rearmed with both Enfield and Springfield rifle muskets.

The battle history of the 12th Illinois was second to none. Beginning at Fort Donelson and continuing through the campaign under General Sherman in Georgia and the Carolinas, it fought with valor and distinction.

SONS OF ERIN

It was midmorning on September 17, 1862, near the town of Sharpsburg, Maryland. The battle of Antietam had been raging for several hours as a brigade of the Army of the Potomac's II Corps moved forward toward the position held by Confederate troops of Gen. D. H. Hill's Division. This brigade, composed of three ethnic Irish regiments—the 63rd, 69th, and 88th New York—along with the 29th Massachusetts, was destined to gain everlasting fame as the Irish Brigade. When the day was done, the Confederate position would also have a name; it would be known forever as the "Bloody Lane."

Leading the brigade was a true son of Erin, Gen. Thomas Francis Meagher, known for his elegant uniforms. At the battle of Savage Station in June, he had worn a suit of dark green velvet, trimmed with gold lace. Today, mounted on a magnificent bay horse with the flags of the 69th New York behind him, he was the picture of glory. The regiment, and indeed the brigade, was uniformed in the eight-button jacket issued by the state of New York. This jacket had been adopted pursuant to the recommendations of a military board appointed by the state in 1861. The men of the color guard were identified by their nonregulation chevrons surmounted by embroidered crossed U.S. flags. The brigade's knapsacks had been stacked in the rear prior to the assault, and a few young soldiers had chosen to remove their shoes and move forward barefoot. Within a short time, the Confederates were driven from their post, but the cost to the Irish Brigade was high: 113 killed and 422 wounded.

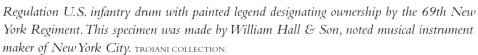

Regulation U.S. infantry drum with painted legend designating ownership by the 69th New York Regiment. This specimen was made by William Hall & Son, noted musical instrument maker of New York City. TROIANI COLLECTION.

41ST NEW YORK VOLUNTEER INFANTRY, DE KALB REGIMENT, 2ND YAEGER REGIMENT

Besides the well-known French Zouave uniform and Highlander's kilt, another distinctive foreign uniform was worn during the Civil War by an American volunteer regiment—the green and red of the German jaeger, or rifleman. German riflemen had traditionally worn green since the eighteenth century. During the American Revolution, German mercenaries had included a Rifle Corps, equipped with short and stubby, but efficient, rifles and uniformed in green coats faced with red.

The 41st was raised mainly from the German-born immigrants of New York State. As one of four regiments that the Union Defense Committee was authorized to recruit and equip, the 41st was exempt from any state regulations as to its uniforms and equipment. The regiment originally was known as the De Kalb Regiment, after German general Johann de Kalb, who was killed in the Patriot cause during the American Revolution. It was also known as the 2nd Yaeger Regiment, as there was already a 1st German Rifles in service under Col. Louis Blenker.

The 41st chose the distinctive green and red of German riflemen for its uniform, which was described in detail by the New York City newspapers:

> The dress consists of a dark green frock coat, trimmed with red on the collars and cuffs, gray pantaloons, trimmed with a red cord, and cloth caps of the same color as the coats faced with red. The troops are also provided with an overcoat of gray pilot cloth, made after the Prussian Army regulation; in fact, the complete outfit of the regiment is on the plan of the Prussian Army. The knapsacks are to be of the most approved style, being sloped, so as to fit in the hollow of the back, and of a size and weight to contain a good store of outfit—the officers' uniforms are precisely the same as that of the men, with the only distinction of their shoulder straps and the lace on their caps.

Armed with M1842 muskets, the regiment was ready for war by June 1861, when it was presented with an American standard of silk with gold fringe. On the blue field was a shield surrounded by thirty-four stars and with the inscription "De Kalb Regiment, N.Y.V." By July, the regiment was paraded with "neat havelocks," which "were found of unusual benefit in keeping the sun off."

The 41st served in the XI Corps of the Army of the Potomac until after Gettysburg, when it was transferred to South Carolina. Reenlisting in 1864, the 41st continued as a veteran regiment, fighting in the Shenandoah Valley at Cedar Creek and mustering out at City Point after serving in the siege of Petersburg.

DICK AND M. E. CLOW

DE KALB ZOUAVES, 41ST NEW YORK VOLUNTEER INFANTRY, 1861

The 41st New York was raised mainly among the German-American immigrants of New York. Recruited and equipped by the Union Defense Committee of New York City, it was free to design its own uniforms. Most of the regiment, known as the De Kalb Regiment after Revolutionary War hero Johann de Kalb, a Prussian general who gave his life in the winning of U.S. independence, chose green rifle coats trimmed with red like those of Prussian jaegers, or riflemen. The regiment was also known as the 2nd Yaeger Regiment, because Blenker's 8th New York was already called the 1st German Rifles, but like the 8th, it had to content itself with M1842 muskets rather than rifles. It was not until 1863 that these riflemen received M1861 rifle muskets.

Even with its Germanic heritage, the 41st could not resist the influence of that French craze—the Zouave uniform. The regiment's Company A was known as the De Kalb Zouaves or Duysing's Zouaves, after its captain, and wore "a dark blue jacket (braided with red) and pantaloons with the yellow and black leggings of the Turcos, the blue sash and the red fez and blue tassel" like the French Zouaves. The elaborate yellow trim on the sleeve was not, however, a part of the French uniform, and is found on an original jacket in the collection of the Smithsonian Institution.

By 1862, when the regiment served as part of Blenker's division at Cross Keys, Groveton, and Second Bull Run, it was garbed in the blue jackets of New York Volunteers. The regiment participated in the XI Corps' disasters at Chancellorsville and Gettysburg and was in Hilton Head, South Carolina, when its service expired. It mustered out on June 9, 1864. A reorganized veteran 41st went on to the end of the war, seeing action at Cedar Creek and Petersburg, Virginia.

TIM OSTERHELD

BROTHERS OF IRELAND

As Gen. George B. McClellan's Peninsula campaign ground to a halt outside Richmond, the forces of Robert E. Lee were on the offensive. After failing to destroy Union forces at Mechanicsville late in June 1862, Lee pressed the Federal defensive lines near Gaines' Mill. He threw his best at the beleaguered Federals, including Stonewall Jackson's seemingly invincible brigade. Among the first hit were the Irish volunteers of Col. Thomas Cass's 9th Massachusetts Volunteer Infantry.

Seeing the green flag of the 9th, Jackson growled that his men should sweep away "that damned brigade" and threw them at Cass's regiment. The gallant little regiment refused to be swept away and, though it lost men, stubbornly held its ground. Then, just as it seemed about to be overrun, the green flags of the real Irish Brigade came up in relief, as the Irishmen of the 63rd New York joined the Irishmen of the 9th Massachusetts in combat. Together they thwarted Jackson.

Irish green had saved that part of the field. It was seen in the battle flags of both regiments and in the unique green velvet uniform worn by that most Irish of all Irishmen, Gen. Thomas Francis Meagher. Meagher's gaudy outfit was topped off with a green-plumed straw hat. The men of the 9th wore no green, only the standard blue of the Federal soldier. The men of the 63rd New York also wore Federal blue, but they stripped to their multihued shirts in the June heat of Virginia's Peninsula. On that day, all their clothing was begrimed by black powder, smoke, and blood, as these brothers of Ireland held the field.

JOHN KERR

55TH NEW YORK, LAFAYETTE GUARD, 1861

On April 17, 1861, the French-American 55th New York State Militia voted unanimously to offer its services to the national government. It was accepted about the first of May and set up camp on Staten Island to organize for war. But the militia's colonel became hopelessly ensnared in military red tape, and as delays mounted, the regiment began to disintegrate, as whole companies deserted to other volunteer regiments that were leaving for the war. To get the regiment to the front, its officers appealed to Baron Philippe Régis de Trobriand to take the colonelcy and lead the regiment to war.

De Trobriand's regiment, now called the 55th New York Volunteer Infantry, or Lafayette Guard, retained the uniforms of its French heritage: "Regiment will assemble on Wednesday, 31st inst. In fatigue dress (overcoats with epaulettes, red pants, small caps, shoes and gaiters). Armed and equipped with knapsacks containing the necessary underclothing." The New York City firm of Brooks Brothers contracted for uniforms for the regiment, including "60 French Imported Scarlet Fez Caps at $1.25 ea." As there was not sufficient red cloth for the regiment's trousers, Brooks Brothers manufactured "Brown Drilling Pants" as substitutes. At the end of August, the 55th finally went to war, trained and equipped, and drilled by an amateur colonel soon became professional. "They went away in heavy duck pantaloons and blue overcoats, except one company wearing French Zouave uniforms."

De Trobriand's already undersize regiment suffered severely in the Peninsula, and in September 1862, its survivors were consolidated into a four-company battalion. De Trobriand lamented: "Where were the red pantaloons? Where were the Zouave jackets? And above all those who had worn them, and whom we looked in vain among the ranks to find." Within months, the 55th disappeared, consolidated into the 38th New York, with de Trobriand becoming a brigadier general after commanding a brigade in the III Corps.

COLE UNSON

These simple brigadier general's shoulder straps belonged to Philippe Régis Denis de Keredern de Trobriand, an immigrant from France. The embroidered hat insignia dates from his colonelcy with the 55th New York Volunteer Infantry, Lafayette Guard. COLLECTION OF NEW YORK STATE DIVISION OF MILITARY AND NAVAL AFFAIRS.

Cartridge box plate of the 55th New York Volunteers recovered from a camp site in Virginia. Another variation of this type has also been excavated, but with the numbers in script. WEST POINT MUSEUM.

39TH NEW YORK, GARIBALDI GUARD

Almost certainly the most cosmopolitan of all volunteer regiments, the 39th New York Volunteer Infantry was also plagued with the most notorious of colonels. Col. Frederic George D'Utassy gathered a polyglot regiment of Hungarians, Spanish, Italians, French, Swiss, and Germans to form the Garibaldi Guard, or perhaps more appropriately, the 1st Foreign Rifles. D'Utassy's personal history is clouded, but his conduct with his regiment is well documented. Almost immediately his regiment staged a minor mutiny over being issued M1842 muskets rather than the rifles they expected. There was friction between the diverse elements of the regiment, and the inept officers D'Utassy gathered were incapable of instilling discipline. D'Utassy himself was almost immediately under suspicion of having bilked the government by charging for 900 rations when only 700 men were in the regiment. Eventually D'Utassy was court-martialed, found guilty, and sent to New York's Sing Sing Prison for multiple frauds committed against his own regiment and the government.

In the beginning, though, the regiment was cloaked in the romance of its name, uniforms, and multiple national flags. Before they received their full uniforms, the men of the regiment paraded in red Garibaldi shirts, of which it was said that "the warm scarlet color . . . , reflected upon the men's faces as they stood in line, made a picture which never failed to impress the reviewing officer." The regiment's full uniform eventually consisted of "blue frock coats, blue pants trimmed with red cord, red undershirts, and felt hat ornamented with feathers and green leaves. Their knapsacks contained blankets and comfortable under clothing, while the haversacks were crammed with bread, cheese, bologna sausages, etc." Ultimately the 39th shed itself of both its bad officers and distinctive uniforms, becoming one of the Army of the Potomac's steady regiments.

JOHN H. KURTZ

GARIBALDI LEGION, 1861

WILLIAM RODEN

With thousands of immigrants only years, or even months, away from their native land, ethnic pride was very evident in nineteenth-century America. Substantial communities of these new Americans existed, particularly near the various ports of entry from Boston to New Orleans. Many who had come to this country seeking a new life were veterans of European armies. These men, and those who would find a common bond with them, flocked to the colors of their adopted land. Even before war became a reality, companies of militia were being formed that had a distinctive European flavor both in appearance and name. In 1861, the major influx of immigrants of Italian and southern European heritage was still several decades away. By this time, however, both New York and New Orleans could boast substantial numbers of arrivals from Italy. Many of these were followers or admirers of the Italian revolutionary Giuseppe Garibaldi.

When the shooting finally started, both the Union and Confederate armies had within their ranks units of Italian-born volunteers. The Garibaldi Guard, later to become the 39th New York Infantry, served in the Union Army of the Potomac's famed II Corps. In the South, the *New Orleans Bee* reported that a battalion "composed exclusively of Italians," which would be known as the Garibaldi Legion, would be raised in that city and went on to describe in detail the uniform it would wear.

> Hat: high peaked black felt, moderate sized brim turned up on left side with a small bunch of green, black and white feathers . . . around the crown a green silk cord terminating behind in a tassel and fixed in front with a gilt button
> Jacket: a round jacket of red woolen cloth
> Trousers: bottle green pantaloons cut wide and reaching below the knee, there held by gaiters or leggings of the same material buttoned on the outer side
> Accouterments: a black belt and cartridge box

The *New Orleans Daily Picayune* reported on the "dashing red uniforms and plumed hats" of that city's Garibaldi Legion. Although the future of the Southern Garibaldis would be quite different from that of their Northern brothers, the short history of the New Orleans legion would do credit to the ethnic population of that city.

By October 1861, it was reported by another New Orleans newspaper, the *Daily True Delta,* that 30,000 Louisiana troops had been sent out of the state in service of the Confederacy. With New Orleans and the state itself vulnerable to attack, the troops left behind—the volunteer militia, including the flamboyant Garibaldis—would be responsible for their defense. These soldiers likely would have given a good account of themselves if a fight for the city had become a reality. As it was, the city administration elected to surrender on April 29, 1862, rather than face destruction at the hands of Union naval gunboats on the Mississippi. Following the surrender, the Garibaldi Legion ceased to exist as a military organization. Some of the members likely found their way into other Confederate regiments, but their flamboyant uniforms were left behind, along with the short history of the Southern Garibaldis.

NEW YORK INDEPENDENT BATTALION, *LES ENFANTS PERDUS*

This unusual unit was organized in New York City during August and September 1861 from various immigrant groups by Lt. Col. Felix Confort, a former French Army captain. The term *Les Enfants Perdus* seems to have been derived from the Crimean War, when *enfants perdus* referred to groups of soldiers engaged in what might be called a "forlorn hope" task, such as an assault upon an impregnable position or other post of extreme danger. Confort's men were supposedly "intended for special service as tirailleurs and scouts." Instead, they were first engaged in McClellan's bungled Peninsula campaign, where they were described as "foreigners, the rough-scuff of New York City," and it was noted that "some twenty tried to desert to the enemy after the first pay day." Assigned later to the XVIII Corps, *Les Enfants'* most active service came in the siege of Battery Wagner, South Carolina, and Morris Island.

The first uniform was a triple-breasted chasseur-style coat with yellow trim and a detachable yellow plastron. It was described in 1861 as "an improvement on the well known Zouave costume. The trousers are not so baggy, the jacket has short tunic lapels and the cap is of the kepi instead of the fez pattern. In color the uniform is throughout, dark blue, trimmed with yellow; is made of serviceable cloth, and will wear well, at the same time it looks so handsome." According to a later description, it was a "smart blue tirailleur uniform with yellow breast pieces, shoulder knots and facings, and the rakish 'plume de coq' which garnished their hats, gave them a decidedly foreign appearance." A later uniform was made "without plastroon [*sic*] (or yellow front piece) and substituting in lieu of the three rows of round buttons, one row of 9 New York State buttons—Trimmings of Infantry Blue instead of Yellow as present." Fancy dress, however, does not make a soldier, and *Les Enfants* never matched the brilliance of their uniforms.

DR. DAVID YANKE

CLEAR THE WAY

All regiments of the Irish Brigade suffered severely on the bloody day at Antietam, their ranks thinned and their flags shredded. In November 1862, the 28th Massachusetts, an Irish-American regiment in the IX Corps, exchanged places with the Yankee 29th Massachusetts of the Irish Brigade. Thus, on the coming bloody day in December, the Irish Brigade would be composed fully of Irish-American regiments.

At Fredericksburg, Virginia, on the cold morning of December 13, 1862, cloaked in sky blue great coats, their dark blue forage caps pulled tightly down on their heads, the men of the Irish Brigade were deployed in a sunken road bordered by a thick stone wall. They were about to make a desperate assault, and their precious green battle flags were gone, sent home for replacement. Only the new 28th had unscathed colors to take onto the field of battle. As Gen. Thomas F. Meagher gave a fiery oration, his staff officers handed out sprigs of green boxwood for the men's caps. The Irish Brigade would go into battle under green colors, even if most of its regiments lacked their flags.

In the noise of battle, the Irish cheer "Faugh-a-Ballagh!" was heard from the 28th: "Clear the Way!" It was the regimental motto. Yet despite all their courage, the wearing of the green, and the regimental motto, the Irish Brigade could not overcome the sheets of flaming lead that tore through their ranks. Their gallant assault upon the Confederates at Fredericksburg failed. No dead were closer to the Confederate lines than those of the 28th and the other regiments of the Irish Brigade.

Forage cap of the 63rd New York Volunteers, which formed part of the Army of the Potomac's famed Irish Brigade. The cap bears the red trefoil badge of the 1st Division, II Army Corps, with the regimental number and company letter. COLLECTION OF NEW YORK STATE DIVISION OF MILITARY AND NAVAL AFFAIRS.

IRISH BRIGADE BAND

By August 1862, the famed Irish Brigade had not been at war for a year, but its commander, Gen. Thomas F. Meagher, was in New York City to recruit new men for his brigade. His task had been made easier by the members of the Produce Exchange, who appropriated money for a bounty of $10 each to the first 300 recruits for the brigade. Along with the state and Federal bounties, this meant that a recruit would receive about $140 on joining his regiment. The recruits took a new brigade band along with them to the war. A reporter for the *Irish-American* described the scene as Meagher left for Harrison's Landing with recruits and the new band: "The new band for the Brigade went out with Gen. Meagher in the *Key West*. They are under the leadership of Edward Manahan. The members wear a tasteful gray uniform faced with green, and make a handsome appearance. They will be a great addition to the Brigade, and will cheer the tedium of camp life with some of the fine old music of Fatherland, to which every true Celt is so passionately attached."

With less than a year's service, the Irish Brigade had already fought at Fair Oaks, Gaines' Mill, Savage Station, White Oak Swamp, and Malvern Hill. Still ahead were Antietam, Fredericksburg, Chancellorsville, and Gettysburg. The Celts of the Irish Brigade would have reason to seek comfort in music in the long, sad months ahead.

DR. COYLE S. CONNOLLY

PRIVATE, 45TH NEW YORK INFANTRY, JULY 1863

The 45th New York Infantry can be considered one of the very best of the ethnic German regiments to serve in the Union army. Recruited in New York City as the 5th German Rifles, and mustered in September 9, 1861, the regiment was made up entirely of immigrant Germans. Orders were given in the native tongue, and until forbidden by the army, the regimental books were written in German. The early regimental assignments were varied and included time in the Union Army of Virginia under Maj. Gen. John Pope. By September, the 45th was part of the 1st Division of the Army of the Potomac's XI Corps.

The arms and uniform of the 45th New York were, as befitted their German ancestry, carefully documented in the meticulously kept regimental books. In January 1862, the following accounting was made of the regimental ordnance:

737 - Remington rifles, Cal. 54
88 - Enfield rifles, Cal. 577
733 - Sword bayonets for Remington rifles
735 - Sword bayonet scabbards, Remington rifles
88 - Sword bayonets, Enfield rifle
48 - Swords, N.C.O.
133 - Belts & Plates, N.C.O.
622 - Belts & Plates, privates, N.Y.
95 - Belts & Plates, U.S.
832 - Cartridge boxes
832 - Cap pouches
832 - Frogs

The men of the 45th New York wore the state-issued jacket into the Gettysburg campaign. By direction of the commander of the XI Corps, each soldier was ordered to carry two pairs of shoes. The men were also directed "to take on the march, overcoats, India Rubber Blanket, and Shelter tent." It was left to the discretion of the regimental commander whether the men would also carry woolen blankets.

The 45th New York was thrown into the fighting north of Gettysburg on July 1 and made a heroic stand in the streets of the town during the retreat of the XI Corps. The regiment would continue to serve in the XI and later the XX Corps until July 1864, when it was ordered to the defense of Nashville and consolidated with the 58th New York.

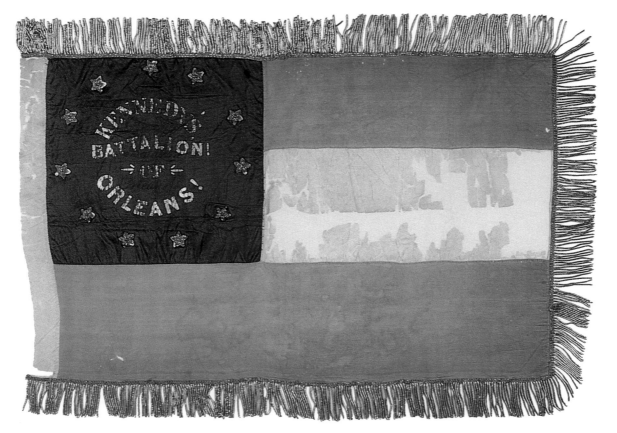

One of a pair of the first national Confederate guide flags of the 5th Louisiana Battalion (later Kennedy's 21st Louisiana Volunteers). These small silk banners, measuring 31 1/2 by 18 1/2 inches, were stationed on the flanks of the regimental line to aid the men in keeping proper alignment. The 5th Battalion served at Island Number 10, the battle of Belmont, and in operations around Corinth. This small unit was composed almost exclusively of German immigrants, with a sprinkling of French, Belgians, and Scandinavians. TROIANI COLLECTION.

SOURCES

VOLUNTEERS OF MANY NATIONS

INTRODUCTION

1. Frederick P. Todd, *American Military Equipage, 1851–1872,* vol. 2 (n.p.: Chatham Square, 1983).
2. *Washington, D.C., Evening Star,* May 30, 1861.
3. Maj. Robert Taylor, Inspector 4th Brigade, October 25, 1859 report, in *Annual Report* (Albany, 1860).

IRISH JASPER GREENS, LANCE CORPORAL, FALL 1861

Savannah Morning News, November 30, 1927.

Georgia Historical Society, Savannah, Irish Jasper Greens Papers, vol. 2, Rules and Minutes, January 31, 1856–January 30, 1862; and box 3, folder 8, Property Returns, 1861.

COMPANY K, 69TH NEW YORK STATE MILITIA

Washington, D.C., Evening Star, Thursday, May 23, 1861.

Irish American, August 17, 1861.

New York State Archives, *Commissary General of Ordnance for 1861,* Reports, 91.

Michael Cavanaugh, *Memoirs of General Thomas Francis Meagher,* Worcester, Mass.: Messenger Press, 1892.

8TH AND 20TH NEW YORK VOLUNTEER INFANTRY, 1861

C. Eugene Miller, *Der Turner Soldat: A Turner Soldier in the Civil War, Germany to Antietam* (Louisville, Ky: Calmar Publications, 1988).

79TH NEW YORK HIGHLANDERS, 1861

Military Gazette, September 15, 1860, 277.

William Todd, *The 79th Highlanders, New York Volunteers in the War of the Rebellion, 1861–1865* (Albany, N.Y.: Branlow, Burton, and Co.), 1886.

12TH ILLINOIS INFANTRY, 1ST SCOTTISH REGIMENT

National Archives, Record Group 94, Order Book, 12th Illinois Infantry.

SONS OF ERIN

Frederick P. Todd, *American Military Equipage,* (Providence, R.I.: Company of Military Historians, 1977), 2:358.

41ST NEW YORK VOLUNTEER INFANTRY, DE KALB REGIMENT, 2ND YAEGER REGIMENT

Ron Field and Roger Sturcke, "41st New York Volunteer Infantry Regiment, (De Kalb Regiment or 2nd Yaeger Regiment) 1861–1865," *Military Collector and Historian* 39, no. 2 (summer 1987): 76, 77.

New York Herald, June 9, 1861, 5.

New York Daily News, June 20, 1861, 8.

New York Herald, July 4, 1861, 8.

DE KALB ZOUAVES, 41ST NEW YORK VOLUNTEER INFANTRY, 1861

New York Tribune, June 8, 1861, 8.

National Archives, Record Group 156, Ordnance Returns, U.S. Regiments, 41st New York Volunteer Infantry.

Frederick Phisterer, *New York in the War of the Rebellion, 1861–1865,* vol. 3 (Albany, N.Y.: J. B. Lyon, 1912), 2237–38.

BROTHERS OF IRELAND

Alonzo Foster, *Reminiscences and Record of the 6th New York V.V. Cavalry* (privately printed, 1892), 35.

55TH NEW YORK, LAFAYETTE GUARD, 1861

Régis de Trobriand, Four Years in the Army of the Potomac (Boston: Ticknor, 1889).

New York Evening Express, July 29, 1861, 3.

New York Tribune, September 1, 1861, 5.

Brooks Brothers contract, August 3, 1861.

39TH NEW YORK, GARIBALDI GUARD

Ella Lonn, *Foreigners in the Union Army* (Baton Rouge: Louisiana State University Press, 1951).

William L. Burton, *Melting Pot Soldiers* (Ames, New York: Fordham University Press, 1988).

New York Herald, May 29, 1861, 8.

GARIBALDI LEGION, 1861

New Orleans Bee, January 28, 1861.

New Orleans Daily Picayune, June 11, 1861.

New Orleans Daily True Delta, October 20, 1861.

NEW YORK INDEPENDENT BATTALION,
LES ENFANTS PERDUS

New York Herald, December 7, 1861.

Irish-American, March 22, 1862.

Francis Balace and John R. Elting, "Les Enfants Perdus, 1861–1864," *Military Collector and Historian.* 22, no. 1 (spring 1970): 26–27.

National Archives, Record Group 92, entry 999, vol. 20, 423.

CLEAR THE WAY

Capt. O. P. Conyngham, *The Irish Brigade and Its Campaigns* (1867; reprint, Baltimore: Butternut and Blue, n.d.), 341.

IRISH BRIGADE BAND

Irish-American, August 16, 1862.

Joseph G. Bilby, *Remember Fontenoy: The 66th New York and the Irish Brigade in the Civil War* (Hightstown, N.J.: Longstreet House, 1995).

William F. Fox, *Regimental Losses in the American Civil War* (Albany, N.Y.: Albany Publishing Co., 1889).

PRIVATE, 45TH NEW YORK INFANTRY, JULY 1863

National Archives, Record Group 393, entry 5323, Special Orders XI Corps, Order's No. 68, April 14, 1863.

New York Monument Commission, *New York at Gettysburg,* vol. 1 (Albany, N.Y.: J. B. Lyon, 1900), 375–81.

Frederick H. Dyer, *A Compendium of the War of the Rebellion,* vol. 3 (New York: Thomas Yoseloff, 1959).